Guaranteed Results!
The information you need to increase your sales and improve your business.

If after reading this book and implementing 10 ideas you do not have an increase in sales, return the book and your sales receipt to Robinson & Associates for a complete refund.

Martin R. Baird

A Robinson & Associates Book

▼▼▼▼▼ GUARANTEED RESULTS ▼▼▼▼▼

Cover Design by Vince Schwartz, Lulham & Black, Creative Director

GUARANTEED RESULTS. Copyright ® 1994 by Martin R. Baird, 12629 North Tatum Blvd., Suite 237, Phoenix, Arizona 85032 U.S.A. All rights reserved. Printed in the United States of America. No part of this book may be used or reproduced, stored in a retrieval system, or transmitted in any form or by any means, electronical, mechanical, photocopying, recording or otherwise, except for brief quotations in reviews, without the prior written permission of the publishers.

Library of Congress Catalog Card No. 94-092364
ISBN 0-964-31340-5 13.95

GUARANTEED RESULTS

Thank You This book is dedicated to my mom and dad, my wonderful wife and our two girls. I would also like to thank my family, my friends and all of the people that have helped me throughout my life. Without all of you, this never would have been possible. Thank you! I hope you like it!

▼▼▼▼▼
GUARANTEED RESULTS
▼▼▼▼▼

Thank You 3
Preface 8
Introduction 10
Don't Try To Be All Things To All People 14
Focus 14
Ad Reprints 19
Added Values or
Value Added Services 19
Advertising 20
All Customers Are Important 20
Articles 21
Backgrounder 22
Banners and Signage 23
Be Helpful and Ask Questions 23
Be Honest With All of Your Marketing Efforts 24
Be Repetitive - Once Is Never Enough 25
Be Realistic on Cost Projections 25
Be an Expert 26
Birthday Reminders 27
Bounce Back Cards 27
Breadth of Services 28
Brochures 29
Business Cards 30
Buttons 31
Buying Media and NOT Waste 31
Call Your Customers 32
Catalogs/Home Shopping 33
Classes - Education 34
Classified Advertising 35
Co-op Programs 35
Cold Calling 37
Competition 37
Create Profitable Packages 38
Create Urgency 39
Define Your Customer 40
Develop A Charity Event 41
Develop A List Of Common Objections And How To
Overcome Them 41
Develop a Marketing Budget 42

▼▼▼▼▼ GUARANTEED RESULTS ▼▼▼▼▼

Direct Mail 43
Direct Selling 45
Discounts 46
Don't Just Follow Your Competition - Be A Leader 47
Drawings 47
Drop Box or Suggestion Box 48
Dropouts and Free Standing Inserts - FSI, Tip-Ins 49
Educate Your Employees 49
Expect To Do More 50
Express Service 51
Frequency Builder 51
Gift Certificates 52
Gift Ideas Throughout Your Business 53
Going To Trade Shows Or Being In A Trade Show 53
Guarantee 54
Have fun 55
Have Your Own Trade Show 56
If You Build A Better Mouse Trap They Will Beat A Path To Your Door. This is a LIE 56
Incentives- Internal and External 57
Incremental Sales 58
Joint or Cross Promotion 59
Joint Venturing 60
Know What Your Customers Like and Dislike 61
Licensing 61
Lifetime Value of Customers 62
Local Personalities or Celebrities to Visit 63
Make Good Customer Service a Priority 63
Make Your Message Consistent 64
Make Your Products Festive 65
Make Promotions and Sales Prominent 66
Make the Customer Your Number One Priority 67
Media/Public Relations 68
Networking 69
New Products/Service Introductions 70
Newsletter 70
On-hold Messages 71
Open Displays 72
Open House 72
Parade of Products and Services 73

▼▼▼▼▼ GUARANTEED RESULTS ▼▼▼▼▼

Phone-In Contests 74
Plan What You Expect The Return To Be From Your Marketing Investment 74
Price 75
Provide A List Of Best Or Most Popular Items To Buy 76
Public Speaking Engagements... 76
Putting Your Sales Messages On Everything 77
Radio Ads... 77
Remember, It's Five Times More Expensive To Get A New Customer Than It Is To Keep A Current One...................... 79
Remember That Everything Your Company Does Affects Your Marketing 79
Radio Remote Broadcasts 80
Run Your Business The Way Your Customers Want It!...... 81
Sales Reps 82
Selling The Back-End... 83
Seminars 83
Start a Data Base 85
Start Marketing and Don't Ever Stop 86
Start Promotions Early 86
Stickers... 87
Suggestive Selling.. 87
Surveys and Questionnaires 88
Telemarketing.. 89
Telephone Answering Scripts 89
Ten Arounds 90
Testing 90
Thank You Notes and Letters 91
Tracking and Monitoring 92
Traffic Patterns 92
Trial Size and Sampling 93
Two-for 94
Use Shoppers 95
Value Packaging... 95
Watch Trends... 96
When You Talk To Your Customers, Always Describe The Benefits, Not The Features... 97
Work With Your Community 97
Yellow Pages.. 98
80/20 Rule.. 99

GUARANTEED RESULTS

Questions 100
When Should I Advertise? 100
What Can I Do To Make My Ads Work Better? 101
How Do I Get A write-up In My Local Newspaper? 102
What Is The Difference Between Marketing And
Advertising? 103
How Do You Know If You Need An Advertising Agency? 104
What Does An Advertising Agency Do For Me? 105
Can I Negotiate Advertising Space Rates? 106
If You Only Had $50 To Spend On Advertising What Would
You Do? 106
How Do I Get People To Come Into My Business? 107
What Should I Budget For Advertising/Marketing? 108
Should I Use Expiration Dates On My
Promotional Offers? 109
How Do I Create Urgency? 109
What Is The Best Way To Cold Call? 110
What Are The Most Important Parts Of Marketing? 111
What Do You Do When People Call Or Stop In And Ask
Price? 112
How Do We Get People In During Our Slow Times? 112
What Do You Do With Angry Customers? 113
Implementation Form 116

GUARANTEED RESULTS

Preface Welcome to *Guaranteed Results*. This book was developed specifically for you. If you have ever said, "How can I increase my sales? What can I do to improve my marketing? Why doesn't my advertising work? How can I make the letters I write more effective?" *Guaranteed Results* is just what you have been looking for. In talking with people like yourself, they told us that they want answers to these questions. But they do not want a marketing text book. They want a book that provides ideas and examples that can be implemented immediately. People want to increase sales and make others aware of products and services so they can buy them. This book was written for that specific reason.

I work with people every day that want their businesses to grow. They are continually looking for new ways to increase their sales. *Guaranteed Results* provides over 100 examples of marketing tools that everyone can use. The most important thing to keep in mind as you read this book is to keep your mind open to the possibilities. You may read about a marketing tool and say, "That is a great idea, but it won't work for my business." The ideas and tools discussed can be used in any business, from retail to service to wholesaling to manufacturing.

We all have a common theme. We are all in business to provide a solution to our customers' problems. We provide that solution with the products and services that we produce. That is the only reason you are in business. If people are not aware of the solution you could be providing them, you will not be in business for long.

As you read along please keep in mind that the examples can work for any business in any location. Many of the examples used are for retail businesses but that does not mean they will not work just as well in

GUARANTEED RESULTS

other situations. All of the examples can and have been applied and used very successfully in business to business applications as well.

Please take your time and read this book from beginning to end. Look at all of the different marketing tools that you could be using. Read the question and answer section at the end. Then keep it around and refer to it when you are looking for ideas or when you want to get a little marketing jump start.

I hope *Guaranteed Results* introduces you to many new marketing tools and also serves as a reminder that utilizing these tools can help you grow and succeed.

Martin R. Baird

▼▼▼▼▼ GUARANTEED RESULTS ▼▼▼▼▼

Introduction Welcome, I'm Martin R. Baird. We are going to be talking about marketing. One of the things I want to make sure of is that if you have any questions please take a moment and write them in the back of the book in the notes section. You can then either look up the answer or call and ask me. The reason I wrote this book is because of you. I want this to be an educational experience for you; I want you to go out and say, "Boy, I learned something and I'm going to apply what I have learned to my business. I'm going to make it better." So, again, if you have any questions, jot them down in the back of the book so that we can find answers to them. There is no such thing as a stupid question, except a question that is not asked.

I'm going to explain over 100 different marketing tools that anyone and everyone can and should apply to their business.

Some of these may seem basic or simple but they all can help increase your sales.

▼▼▼▼▼
GUARANTEED RESULTS
▼▼▼▼▼

■   ■   ■

■   ■   ■

■   ■   ■

Please take a moment and connect all 9 dots with only 4 straight lines without lifting your pen. If you must, you can see the solution at the end of the book. Don't cheat!

As the puzzle demonstrates, marketing can be very frustrating. Marketing can also be very fun. Once you have learned some of the key points, all of your marketing activities will become easier and more successful. I know that as you read through the examples in this book you will get ideas and from time to time the light bulb in your head will go on and you will say, "Now I know how to do this." That is what I hope you will accomplish from *Guaranteed Results*.

One of the most important parts of your marketing efforts is setting goals. We talk about this in more detail later but it is too important to only be addressed once. You need to set a target for where you want to be, where you want your business to be and then develop a map that will get you there.

Marketing includes distribution, market research, packaging, sales, advertising, promotion, public relations, pricing, design, sales materials, etc. Too many

▼▼▼▼▼ GUARANTEED RESULTS ▼▼▼▼▼

people have in their mind that marketing is one thing. For example, "I need to run an ad tomorrow, so I can have sales the next day." If it were that simple, you would be a millionaire and I would be out of a job. It takes time, practice and developing the best marketing tools for your business.

For example, one company may generate millions of dollars in sales utilizing direct mail advertising only. That does not mean that every business should stop doing every other form of marketing and only use direct mail. That would be the same as a carpenter that only used a screw driver. It would work well for screws but it would not do a very good job of sanding a table. One of the easiest ways to improve your marketing is to just use the best tool for the job. Everything you do, every way you interact with your key public, is your marketing. So, it's important that you look at all of those as your marketing efforts. Key publics are the people that are most likely to need your products or service. They could also be referred to as your target market, most likely customer or other marketing terms. **Marketing, very simply, is communicating the benefits of your products or services to your customers and potential customers.** Some people say that it is a continuous process of educating your customers about the benefits that you offer them. The key point of this definition of marketing is "communicating the benefits". As you look at other people's marketing, you are going to see many people communicating features. Features don't sell--benefits do. When you look at your business, you have to sit down and say, "What are the benefits?" Features are easy. A vacuum cleaner has a nine amp motor. Who cares? The nine amp motor means that it's going to pick up more dirt. People buy it because it picks up more dirt. When you talk to prospective clients,

GUARANTEED RESULTS

prospective buyers of your product or service, you want to relay the information in a benefit form that they understand. When you say, "My product has X capabilities." What does that mean to them? Put the information in forms that your customers understand and can relate to. For example; Makes them look better; makes their life easier--that's what sells. That's what gets people to say, "I have to have it." They recognize an immediate need or desire. An important item to remember when you start your marketing is to find who you're trying to reach. Too many times' companies don't do that. Say, for example, you're a one hour processing lab and you say, "I'm trying to reach anybody who has film." Well, is that truly the case? Or, are you trying to reach people who have film who want it processed quickly? Think about it--because those are the things that you have to sell. That's the positioning that you can develop that makes you better than or different from a competitor and provides a reason to purchase from you rather than the person or company down the street.

▼▼▼▼▼ GUARANTEED RESULTS ▼▼▼▼▼

Don't Try To Be All Things To All People

It is amazing--when I go into a business or talk with a business person and they want to be everything to everyone. When you do that, you become a jack-of-all-trades and a master of none. You can't do that. Select the people you want to work with; figure out the products and services that they need; and, offer it the best way you possibly can. That way they're going to come back. I see articles and books that say this is "profit motivated marketing." I think this is very funny, because if you're marketing isn't profit motivated, why are you doing it? Are you doing it because your brother is in the advertising business and he gets a commission on all the advertising that you purchase? The reason we are marketing is that we want more sales, and we want our sales to be more profitable. Thus, everything we do from a marketing perspective has to be profit motivated marketing. We are business people. We provide a product or service but, if we do not make a profit, we're not going to be around to offer that product or service. How can we stay around and just keep throwing bad money after good?

Focus

Who are your customers and what do they want? When I say that--when I talk about your customer--you should be able to describe your customer like your best friend. You should know where they go to dinner; what kind of movies they like; how old they are; how much money they make; everything you can know about these people is going to make you a better, more effective marketer. Unless you know them, how can you satisfy their needs? Unless you know their wants, likes and dislikes, how can you

▼▼▼▼▼ GUARANTEED RESULTS ▼▼▼▼▼

possibly say, "This is for you."? You <u>must</u> really know who your customer is.

Ben Franklin said, "People don't plan to fail, they fail to plan." It's absolutely true. I am sure if I asked the readers of *Guaranteed Results*, many of you would say, "Well, I think I would like my sales to be somewhere around $$$$ this year." Set a number and work backwards from it. What am I going to do to get to that number; what am I going to do to get there? Then plan backwards. Because if you don't, you're just going to keep struggling because you are working on something that doesn't exist; it's not hard; it's not tangible. We add to Ben Franklin's quotation, "Many people plan, but more of them fail to implement." People are going to put down this book all over the country and say, "I just read some great marketing ideas. I'm going to apply them. I'm going to put together a plan too." Then the plan ends up as a paper weight or desk ornament. All your plan does is sit at the end of the desk, or on the shelf or wherever. It does not have to be complex. There are software programs out there that make it very, very easy to write one. The Small Business Administration will help you write one. The Service Corp. Of Retired Executives, SCORE, will help you write one. There are many, many organizations that will help you write a simple plan. This document is for you. Don't write it for a marketing person. Do not write it for your banker. Don't write it for your accountant. Write it for yourself. Write it so you can sit down and say, "Hey, I have set an objective and I'm working towards that objective every day." Because if you create the plan and don't implement it, again, you're just wasting time. Your time is too precious to waste.

Some of you are going to be saying throughout this book, "I know that." "I've heard that before." Or, "I read that in a magazine." Or, "I saw that on a video tape."

▼▼▼▼▼ GUARANTEED RESULTS ▼▼▼▼▼

Every time you say that, I want you to stop and think and ask yourself, "But am I implementing it?" Because out of these marketing tools that you will read about, unless you implement them--they are no good. I guarantee that if you implement these tools, your business will move forward. What you have to do is take those handfuls that work for you, work best for your company, in your town, in your situation and start applying them. NOW!

After you have found the tools that work best for you start looking at ways that will make them work better. If you get most of your business from direct mail and you currently get a 3% response, look for a way to improve the response to 5% or 10%.

I would like to ask you four questions. I would like you to write down the answers on the back of a sheet of paper or in the back of the book under "notes". Three of these questions have been asked repeatedly and eighty percent of the people asked get two out of the three wrong. You can get better odds than this in Las Vegas.

First question--this is the one everyone should get right--your name. Yes, I know you are probably snickering. Number two: For those of you who have employees, who pays your employees? And number three: Who do you work for? Those three questions should be very, very simple. Your name--I'm sure you will get that right. Who pays your employees is very simple. It's the person who stands across from you at the cash register and hands you money for your goods or service. Not you! It's the person standing across the counter. Your customer--your customer pays your employees. Most of you are going to nod and say, "Oh, I know what the next answer is too." It's your customer. That's who you work for. All too often we forget that the only reason we have a business--is because of our customers. Because of the person that comes in and

▼▼▼▼▼ GUARANTEED RESULTS ▼▼▼▼▼

spends money with you. Without your customers, unless you have a big bank account that you want to go downhill rapidly, you are not going to make it. You always have to look at everything you do from your customer's perspective. It's not what you want--it's what they want. It's not what you want to sell, it is what they want to buy. When you think of marketing, it's not: "I want to get you to buy two more of my widgets." It's: "What can I provide that my customer wants?" Then they will buy it. How can I present it so it's in a way that they say, "I do need that!" That's what they are there for. Whenever you're thinking about your marketing or whenever I am talking about marketing-- always put it in that perspective. It's what your customers want. Don't do it because you want to, do it because they want it.

Did you get all three of them right? If you did, congratulations. If not, you are like most people. You may have needed to be reminded of how important customers are. I am going to ask you one more question. Why are you reading this book? I hope it's because you want to increase your sales and increase your profits. Because that's what your marketing is there to do. If you are not looking at your marketing as a way of increasing your sales and increasing your profits, I do not know why you're reading this book. Always think of it in that way. (Whenever someone says, "What are you going to do?" Or, "I need a reaction.") Too many times' people do marketing because they need a reaction. They say, "I need a sale right now." Well, you should have thought about that a couple of months ago, because that's often how long it takes to generate a sale. You must also look at marketing tools that you can start using today that may generate incremental sales. For example, when someone is purchasing your product, ask them if they need

▼▼▼▼▼ GUARANTEED RESULTS ▼▼▼▼▼

something else that goes with it. An example that we can all relate to is the fast food industry. They have pioneered and perfected the add-on sale. "Would you like fries with your order?"

I am going to go through this wonderful list of marketing tools. They are in alphabetical order for one simple reason: Every one of you is different. Every one of you has different needs. Every one of you is at a different level in your business. Thus, it would have made it very, very difficult to say, "This is the most important one." Every one of these is important and every one of these is going to be important to you at a different level. Make note of it in the book or try to take a mental note of: "Hey, that one works for me today.", "That one I may be able to use tomorrow.", and "I do not know if I'll ever be able to do this one." At least you are seeing it. The more marketing tools we have at our disposal, the better job we can do with them. I look at all of these tools from a marketing perspective--they are tools that help us to better meet our clients' needs. You are a carpenter. Yes, you can hammer in a nail with a wrench. It just is not the best way to do it. So let's get the best possible tool to fit your marketing needs. What are you trying to accomplish and let's work on one of these that works out very, very well for you. Some of these are going to be so simple, you are going to say, "Yes, I can do that." Well, great! The important part is that you actually do it.

Let the list begin. Please remember there are pages in the back for you to make notes and to write down good ideas that you have while you are reading.

Open up your mind, think outside the box, and have fun!

GUARANTEED RESULTS

Ad Reprints Every time you run an ad, get reprints of it. Have them around the store; have them wherever you're going to be; hand them out. Print specials on coupons on the reverse side. You should also include where they can purchase your product or service. If you are having a sale or you had something in the paper, show it to people. Let them find out about it and talk to them about it. Use the vehicles that you have available and maximize their impact. Many times you can take an ad reprint and have an informative article printed on the back and now people want a copy for the information. You could write the article or maybe you want the credibility of a third party article. Ad reprints provide you with added impact at very little cost--many times you can get them for free from the publications or at least inexpensively.

Added Values or Value Added Services Value added services are something you just can't do without, unless you are the low price volume leader--and that's all you want to be. Value added services are what you do to make you stand out from your competition based on something other than price. Maybe it's throwing in delivery and pick-up. Maybe it's providing an extra battery with a widget. Whatever it is, it does not necessarily have to be a product. Maybe it's providing training--perhaps you have a one hour lab and you say, "People are bringing in bad film, so it makes the prints look bad." Well, bring in a local photographer to come in and do an hour of training on how to use a 35 millimeter camera; or work with a widget store. There are many opportunities for you to add value to the service or product you have to sell, and usually it will

GUARANTEED RESULTS

not cost you any money and you do not have to discount. One of the things I see over and over and over is people saying, "Well, I don't want to do coupons; I don't want to discount; I don't want to do this or that or the other." This gives you an opportunity not to do that, because you can add value that differentiates you from your competitor. All of your competitors are selling basically the same products and services you are. Your value added services give people the perception that you have more for them.

Advertising I recommend advertising, though it's not for everyone. If you know who you are trying to reach and there is a medium that reaches them--whether it be print, radio, outdoor, television, newsletters--if it targets them and it reaches them...do it. The one thing I would say about advertising to everyone reading this is you have to be careful of waste. Too many times an advertising sales rep comes in to your place of business and says, "Do I have a deal for you. I'm going to reach 800,000 people and every one of them owns a widget. And every one of them can go into your establishment and have their widget fixed." Usually it's not true. Usually the 800,000 people are in the total city or the total area, and not everyone is going to drive to your location. Hence, be very, very careful when you are buying advertising. Buy it for the right reasons-- not because the person was an excellent sales person, but because your customer or your potential customer reads that publication, listens to that radio station and watches that television station. Then they will be interested in your business. If you do not know what your customers read, listen to or watch, ask them!

▼▼▼▼▼
GUARANTEED RESULTS
▼▼▼▼▼

All Customers Are Important

Recently I was walking through a trade show wearing jeans and a T-shirt--I looked like a twelve year old. I am standing at a booth trying to get information for my portrait studio. Four gentlemen came up at different times--suits and ties, gray hair--business people--I could not get help. The person would work with these older business people and I did not exist. Well, they did not know I was a speaker; they did not know that I own a portrait studio. I still could have been--and will not be now--a customer. They do not know whether I could have bought one of what they were selling or a thousand of what they were selling. You have to keep the same thing in mind. Just because the person is wearing shorts and a T-shirt doesn't mean they are not going to buy a lot of what you have to sell. Many people dress differently and they act differently. They spend a lot of money. Moral: Do not pre-judge. Everyone who comes in your door is a customer and has a potential to be a good customer. Treat them like one.

Articles

Write articles; publish articles; submit articles; anything you can do with an article, if well done, helps you earn credibility. These articles can be submitted to local, regional or national publications depending on your market. You can submit them to your newspapers, magazines, business publications, retail publications even newsletters that are sent to your market. Work with your suppliers to develop articles. If you work with major companies in your industry write a joint article with them. They can add credibility to your article. Get two paragraphs from someone at one of those companies and two paragraphs from yourself and a photograph about your company and the industry and

▼▼▼▼▼ GUARANTEED RESULTS ▼▼▼▼▼

send it in to the local newspapers, magazines--anywhere you can get a pick-up. Yes, later on in this book it's going to say get reprints of the article. Those articles give you so much credibility. Anytime you are in print and it does not appear that you have paid for it--people believe it's editorial and if people believe it's editorial, they believe it to be fact. No matter what you wrote about, they think it's fact. So write articles--again, it's one of those things where people will put down the book saying, "I can do an article on this, this, this and this." You need to start on them today. You just have to put it into your schedule of "I'm going to do it". If you do not have the time or do not feel comfortable writing, hire an outside person to do it; have someone else do it; but just start writing them. This differentiates you from your competition. If you can write an article that has good information in it, people read it and say, "Wow. They know what they're doing. They know what they're selling." It gives you an excellent advantage over your competition.

Backgrounder Develop a backgrounder or biography on the company as well as yourself and other key people in the company. A backgrounder is background information that you will want and need for the media to use when you submit articles or are going to be interviewed. You want to include all the important who, what, when, where, why and how information. This information is kept by media people for when they need information about a specific topic. Many times you will see and hear people interviewed when a big news story breaks. You will see and hear people being interviewed that are widget experts. These people sent in backgrounders and when the reporter needed information they gave them a call. Most of the time you will not see

▼▼▼▼▼
GUARANTEED RESULTS
▼▼▼▼▼

immediate response from your backgrounder but it is important to do and should cost you very little time and money to complete.

Banners and Signage   At trade shows and in retail stores there are banners and signs everywhere. You should have them in your business too. Out front, inside, down the street, in a complementary business--for example, if you sell tires, see if you can put a banner in a business that does oil changes or one that does auto body work. You should be able to work hand in hand with other businesses in your area. And you will put up a sign for them. The type of signage you use can have great impact on the results. Think about Sandwich signs or A-Frames. Banners and signs can now be done very professionally and very inexpensively. You can even do a limited run of banners--you do not have to do a hundred of them or a thousand of them. There are places that will do one and two. It's very cost effective. Here is an idea--why not do them seasonally? Have a spring banner, summer banner, fall banner, holiday banner. Guess what? They are good next year too, unless you put a year on them--so, don't put a year on them. Banners and signage give people a reason to be interested.

We did a marketing campaign for a business introducing a new product. We ran ads in all of the papers and many of the magazines. We used special receipts and we also put messages in all outgoing envelopes. After it was completed everyone agreed that the most effective marketing tool were the signs and banners. People would come in and ask about the product. Do not overlook the results you can get from banners and signage!

▼▼▼▼▼ GUARANTEED RESULTS ▼▼▼▼▼

Be Helpful and Ask Questions

That does not sound like marketing. It sounds like customer service. Marketing and customer service go hand in hand, because if you do one without the other, either way your business is not going to succeed as well as it could. When I say ask questions, again I get back to that scripting idea. If you know the benefits of your product, you can ask questions that lead people to say, "Yes, they have what I need." Develop those questions. Don't ever say--please don't ever say -- "May I help you?" As soon as you say that, ninety-nine percent of the world is just programmed to say, "Just looking. No thank you, just looking." When that happens, you have missed an opportunity. Again, for your marketing to be profitable you cannot miss opportunities. Tell them they have a nice tie; tell them that you like the color of their outfit; tell them something. Break the ice a different way. If you can get them into a process that is in your best interests--meaning they're interested in your product or service, as opposed to: The typical scenario they expect to encounter that goes something like "I'm going to go in; they're going to say 'may I help you'; I'm going to say 'no'; and they're going to walk away like I've offended them." Figure out a way around that. Figure out a way that gets them closer to where you want them to be as opposed to closer to where they want to be. Remember you are in business to help your customers.

Be Honest With All of Your Marketing Efforts

Many people will say, "We will just tell little white lies." I do not believe in that. It's just going to come back to get you whether you have ads that are misleading

▼▼▼▼▼ GUARANTEED RESULTS ▼▼▼▼▼

or articles that are misleading or promotions that are misleading--just do not do it. Over the legal ramifications of misrepresentation, it makes you look bad because people are going to find out. Then it makes the industry look bad and nobody wins. Always be honest. Put things in the most favorable light, but do not lie. If you are trying to have a successful business and a successful career the only way to do that is with honesty and integrity.

Be Repetitive - Once Is Never Enough

One of the things you will notice in this book is that I am repetitive. People learn through repetition and reinforcement. I have reviewed a number of topics thus far, if you have been making notes. I will go over them over and over and try to state them in different ways. The reason for this is, it is important that you learn about these tools. The same is true with a potential customer. They are very busy, they are not concentrating on your message, they are looking at everything else but your message. So when they do see your message, you have to hit them and hit them and hit them and hit them with it. That's why I say these are all tools. The more tools you can hit them with, the better opportunity you have of getting them to say "Hey I have heard of your company once before!" At least they remember it once. So be repetitive. Research indicates that it takes 7 or 8 times before someone remembers seeing or hearing your message once. You can never be too repetitive. Usually we get tired of the marketing tool or campaign long before our clients have been affected by it.

▼▼▼▼▼ GUARANTEED RESULTS ▼▼▼▼▼

Be Realistic on Cost Projections

Be realistic and specific about what your marketing efforts will cost. This is one area where I see many businesses faltering. They go out and say, "I am going to mail postcards. Twenty-two cents to mail them. I will have them printed up over at a quick copy place. That will only cost $100. I'll use my own list--it's no big deal." Well, it's amazing how quickly those 22 cent stamps add up. It's amazing how quickly that $100.00 for the printing adds up. It is also surprising how much time you put into it. When it's all said and done, you go "WOW! That was expensive." So, be very specific. Add everything up. Be honest about it. Again, I see this happen often where clients say, "Well, this did not really count as marketing." You are only lying to yourself. Be honest. Sit down and say, "What is it going to cost?" And "What am I expecting to get as a return?" That way, you can honestly evaluate it. All of your marketing efforts need to be results based. Look at each of your efforts as this is what I am investing and this is what my return should be. Figure out how many widgets you need to sell to break even. That way you can set a realistic goal.

Be an Expert

This is excellent to do, whether you are in a big town or a small town. You can be in any business and at any level in the company. Be an expert for television, radio, print--any media. You need to be knowledgeable in the subject that you are going to be dealing with. You may even want to study some of your industry publications or journals. Look at all the doctors that are now on TV. They are on the morning shows, they are on the news, they are in the paper. They are no different from any other doctor. They went and said, "I am an expert." A television station said, "Good. We'll put you

▼▼▼▼▼ GUARANTEED RESULTS ▼▼▼▼▼

on our station." Now they are nationwide. You can do the same thing. You can go to the local stations and say, "I want to be the expert on widget making--I want to be the expert on how to use a widget." You will do a radio call-in show; you will write articles; you will do whatever. Again, it gives you unbeatable credibility and will remarkably increase the perception of you in your area. Publications, radio stations and TV stations are always looking for people to do that because they have time to fill and if you can build an audience. When you go in, if you say, "There are X number of people who have purchased or would like more information about widgets in our market. Most of these people are doctors and lawyers and people like this--people with money." It's then very easy for them to sell ad time because high-end people are watching and high-end people are a highly sought after demographic with greater disposable income.

Birthday Reminders Always remember that you are working with people. The person on the other side of the desk pays your salary and pays your employees' salary. Send them birthday reminders. Send them reminders. Send them something. Give them an excuse to come back. It can be funny, it can be serious, it can be sentimental, it can be whatever you want it to be, as long as it fits in the perception of what your customer wants your company to be. If they want your establishment to be fun--make it fun, so that every time your customers walk in, they look forward to it because it's fun. When you send out holiday cards and when you send out birthday cards, make them fun. Then people will say, "It's kind of like being there. Well, maybe the next best thing."

▼▼▼▼▼
GUARANTEED RESULTS
▼▼▼▼▼

Bounce Back Cards Bounce back cards are very simple. It means when someone came in, you gave them something that brought or "bounced" them back. You get them all the time. Haircuts: Buy a haircut, we give you this card, you come back in for a free haircut. You get them at McDonalds. You rub off the card that says "Free Big Mac", but you have to use it on your next visit. McDonalds knows that when you come in again, you are going to buy fries or you are going to buy a soft drink.

The same things happen with your customers. If you are selling widgets, bring them back in. Let them buy batteries again. Let them buy product again. Get them back into your place, so that you have an opportunity to solve more problems for your customer.

One of the things that marketing has to be is an opportunity for you to sell. Just think about it: "How can I get in contact with someone, so that I can talk to them; so that I can meet their need; and, so I can let them buy something I have?"

Breadth of Services Develop a complete list of all the products and services you have to offer. I see this often. Customers do not know the services or the products that you can provide. You'll talk to someone and they will say, "Oh, yes. They make widgets." Well, do they also do widget repair? Do they also have their own little widget painting center? Do they also sell parts for your widget or what other options are there? You want the customer or potential customer to come to you, spend money with you. You need to educate them about what

▼▼▼▼▼ GUARANTEED RESULTS ▼▼▼▼▼

you have before you can expect them to come in. If you do not tell them, nobody else is going to. It's pretty simple. No one is going to help you educate your customers about the services that you can provide them. So have the list of services--put it on everything you do. Say, "We do x, y and z." For example: If we were working with a bank we would encourage them to include the information on teller receipts, deposit slips, banners and in monthly statements. The list could include; checking accounts, savings accounts, CD's, IRA's, Credit Cards, Safe Deposit Boxes, Automatic Bill Payment and much more. You do not have to take it down to the most minute detail. Give them the big picture so that when the person walks out, after buying a new widget, they can see other services that you provide. Give them something that says you can also have your widget repaired here; you also can have this; you can also have that. The person has already made the buying decision that they can physically get to your establishment. That's a difficult thing to get, trial. You already have it. Now, tell them they want to come back and why. Your breadth of services lists and cards do that. Your breadth of services list may be a printed list, or on banners or even printed on your envelopes and business cards. What about printing it on your shopping bags? Displaying and presenting your product and service options are only limited by your imagination.

Brochures Have something customers and potential customers can take away. It does not have to be fancy; it does not have to be four color; you do not have to run 400,000 of them. It can be very simple, but, again, be consistent. If everything you do is professional--white shirt, fancy tie, dark suit--make your brochure look that way. That is what your

▼▼▼▼▼ GUARANTEED RESULTS ▼▼▼▼▼

customers are expecting. You can now produce an inexpensive professional looking brochure. Many places now sell pre-printed brochure paper. All you need to do is put your copy on the pages. One other great way to do a brochure inexpensively is to use a colored ink. You can use color and a screen (a lighter version of the same color) and end up with a great brochure that did not cost you a fortune. Most printers offer "free color" days. For example; Monday-Blue, Tuesday-Red, Wednesday-Yellow, etc. Take advantage of these opportunities. A quick note on printers. Find a printer that does good printing at a fare price. As a business person you want a good bank and a great printer. Both of them can help you more than you can imagine.

When you write the copy for your brochure keep in mind that all you want this to do is educate your customers and potential customers about the benefits of the products and services you provide. The brochure needs to address their questions and their needs for your product or service.

Business Cards Have them! I know this sounds kind of simplistic. I am surprised at the number of people who do not have business cards--period. It's not that they do not have them with them or that they just run out. They never had them made. Business cards are a great opportunity. Someone wants to know about your business. You are investing only pennies and they have already shown an interest. It's one of the easiest ways to get someone in the door. Have your phone number on it; have your fax number on it; do not make it too cluttered; make it easy to read. Include your unique selling proposition, why they should buy your widget, or how they will benefit from your widget. If you are a

▼
30

▼▼▼▼▼ GUARANTEED RESULTS ▼▼▼▼▼

Realtor you may want to mention that you sell homes fast. Or you guarantee satisfaction. It can be very, very simple, but have them. I'm amazed at how many people think, "Oh, we don't need those. Our business is all word of mouth." Well, just think of how much easier the word of mouth would be if they could give someone else one of your business cards so they don't have to remember or search for the phone number or the address.

Buttons Buttons can be funny; they can be serious; they can mention a special; they can mention an offer, but they are something that we all look at. Your customers, are attracted to them. They give you an opportunity to get a message across succinctly and they give you an opportunity to remind your customers about something they may have forgotten. You see companies that are marketing driven, doing an excellent job with them saying: "Do not forget the batteries." Wow- -- batteries. Those types of things can be very easily done on a button and can be very effective. These can be very cost efficient for you and very effective. This is just one of the marketing tools that you can add to your mix and start to see or increase in sales. They are simple, but they work as a silent salesperson. You may say, "I'm not in retail, I do not need buttons." Well, you are only looking at half of the picture. What about using buttons to promote internal programs such as sales contests or customer service reminders? These also can be purchased very cost effectively no matter whether you need 2 or 2,000.

GUARANTEED RESULTS

Buying Media and NOT Waste

As mentioned previously under negotiating, remember that when you are negotiating to purchase media, be honest with the sales person, and be aggressive with them. Media is a negotiated item. There is no such thing as hard and fast in media. I guarantee you, if you lock a media sales person in a room long enough, the price will change. You need to be smart about what you are buying. Look at what the cost per thousand (CPM) is, but look at the cost per thousand of your customers, not just against the population. Your customer is specific. Again, just like that friend I talked about at the beginning, you want to be able to know your customer and define them, to the point where you give them a name. When you can picture them in your mind, it's much easier to buy the media without waste because you can say, "Does Chuck (my target person or customer) listen to that station? Does Chuck read that magazine?" Do enough "Chucks" read that magazine? Ask the media sales person. Here's the person I am going after. How many of them read your publication? How many of them listen to your station? How many of them watch your news? If the media salesperson doesn't know, tell them to find out or you will not place your ad. This way you will buy intelligently.

Call Your Customers

Call customers and invite them in or just say "Hello." Too many times you get in a situation where "customer" becomes a generic term. It should not. It should be a very specific term. Someone we relate to very, very well. Call them--what is wrong with just saying "Hi"? "Hi, it's Marty from Widget World. I wanted to say 'Hi, how is everything going? We made 100 widgets

▼
32

▼▼▼▼▼ GUARANTEED RESULTS ▼▼▼▼▼

for you 18 months ago. Those were some great widgets. I hope you are having a good year!"

This creates top of mind awareness. Top of mind awareness simply means that your customer is thinking of you. You do not have to ask them to come in; you do not have to ask them to purchase immediately; you do not have to put them on the spot and make them feel awkward. You can very, very easily just help them to remember you exist. I am shocked at the number of items I have purchased and nobody cares. After I am gone, I feel, "I just spent a thousand dollars and I bet they will never call me." Why not? Why not call me and say, "Hey, there is a new thing that goes with the last thing you purchased." Why not try to get me to visit again? I have already purchased there once. If you did a good job, I should come back in again. So tell me why to come in again. A phone call is an easy way to do that. Select 5 or 10 customers that have not been in recently and call them. By doing this everyday you can see some amazing results.

Catalogs/Home Shopping

Catalogs are one of the fastest growing ways of selling your products or services. People are getting busier and catalogs or home shopping makes it quick and easy. Think of the number of people that are getting catalogs that could be buying your product or service. If you do not have enough products or services for your own catalog you can be in someone else's catalog, often you can buy space or give a percentage of sales to the catalog company for listing your products and services in theirs. If you are considering this, start by trying only one or two products and see how it goes. This may be an excellent way for you to increase your current sales. If you do have enough products and services to do your own

▼▼▼▼▼ GUARANTEED RESULTS ▼▼▼▼▼

catalog, start small, make it look good, and be repetitive. It you want to do your own catalog it can be very expensive. You have the costs of mailing lists, postage, printing, design, photography, copy, etc. They can be time consuming and often very costly. If this is your first attempt at it please start out small and learn smaller lessons.

The newest crazes in this type of selling are the TV home shopping programs. The best way to work with them is to just call them and get your idea in motion. Usually they will request detailed information about your company as well as your product or service. They will want to know quantities that are available as well as pricing. This can be a great way to introduce a new product or to increase distribution of a current product. For many companies this is a good way to increase distribution without the high overhead of retail sales.

Classes - Education

Education is very popular right now--education about anything. Invite the local preschool, daycare center, grade school, junior high school, high school--show them what you do. Kids love it. Teachers have needs that your products or services can fill; the parents have needs that your products or services can fill; the grandparents; the aunts and uncles. It's a wonderful opportunity for you to get your name, your product, your service, your philosophy in front of people. That gives you an opportunity to profit, so put together classes. They do not have to be formal; they do not have to be "Professor So-n-So". They can be very informal; They could even be free; or they could be a profit center. They give you an opportunity to get people in the door and keep them accustomed to the product you provide, the service you provide and how you do things. Use this as an excuse to better educate

▼▼▼▼▼ GUARANTEED RESULTS ▼▼▼▼▼

your customers so they become better consumers of your products and services. When you look in the newspaper you will see more and more classes on everything from investments to cake decorating. Companies do this to generate leads and to introduce more people to their products and services.

Classified Advertising Classified ads are the small ads that are in the back of magazines, in your newspaper or publications that are just classified ads. For many businesses these can be an excellent way to start. They give you the opportunity to increase the exposure of your products and services and it can be done very cost effectively. When you run classifieds you want to think about it just as you would any other advertising--are the people that read this publication my potential customer? If the answer is "no", do not run the ad. If the answer is "yes", you need to start thinking about what the ad needs to emphasize. As always, you want to lead with your strongest benefit or your solution to the reader's problem. If you are in the insurance business you may want a headline that reads, "Lower Monthly Premiums!" or maybe "Earn more than bank CD's!" These get the readers' attention. Do not forget to have your call to action or reason for urgency. Classifieds should be kept short, but you want to make it long enough to tell your story and to get the reader to respond. Once again, classifieds are just like any other marketing tool. You need to test headlines and offers as well as run your ad often enough to generate results.

Co-op Programs How many of you take advantage of co-op programs that exist with

▼▼▼▼▼
GUARANTEED RESULTS
▼▼▼▼▼

your suppliers? For those of you who said "yes", that's good. I'll bet there are many of you who have yet to take advantage of them. Co-op programs promote cooperative marketing between manufacturers and retailers, or companies that can jointly benefit from working together. For those of you who said "no", you are missing out on a great opportunity. Co-op programs are FANTASTIC. Someone is saying, "I will give you money to market your product or service along with mine. It may be the company that produces the products you sell; it may be a company that produces parts for products you sell; it may be a company that services the products you sell. Whomever it is, ask them if they offer a co-op marketing program. If they don't, tell them they have to have one if they want your business. Please start using co-op programs that are available to you. It is like college scholarships. If it is not used every year it just goes to waste! It's an opportunity where suppliers will match your advertising investment--basically doubling your exposure, with no increased cost. Just go to them and say, "I'll put the Widget World logo at the bottom of my ad; I'll put service provided by Widget World in my ads; I'll do what you want to meet your criteria and we both benefit." Excellent, excellent programs. If you do not know about them, ask your sales representatives. If they will not tell you anything, call one of the radio or TV stations in your area. There are books on co-ops broken down like a dictionary listing every company, explaining their co-op program, who to contact, addresses and the key information you need. It is very easy to start doing. To participate in most co-ops, all you have to do is get a pre-approval for the ad then send them a copy of the published ad, a copy of the paid invoice and say, "I want reimbursement." It's not going to happen immediately. They do not like parting

▼▼▼▼▼ GUARANTEED RESULTS ▼▼▼▼▼

with their money any more than you do with yours, but they will pay you.

The reason companies do co-op programs are because the more of their products or services you sell the more money they make. It is cheaper to pay half of the advertising and work with you than it would be to pay all of it themselves. Some aggressive marketing people will have 3 or 4 companies co-oping one ad. By doing this the other companies will pay for most or all of the ad costs. This means a potential for almost free advertising for you!

Cold Calling

Some people enjoy the idea of going to someone they've never met, in a business they've never seen before and saying, "Hi, my name is Marty. I'd like to talk to you about my product or service." Most of us would rather be poked in the eye with a sharp object! Fortunately, there are other ways of cold calling that are not as "cold". Talk to people you know; talk to past customers; talk to anybody who will influence your potential customer, your target market. Talk to these people and say, "Hey, do you know someone who needs X? Do you know someone who needs Y? Did you know we do this and we can do it for...?" It's surprising how many doors this can open. If you have a product that services, for example, hospitals- just call the hospitals and say, "I have a product that helps you reduce your costs!"

I do cold calling, from time to time. It's not my favorite thing to do in the world, but it's amazing how many opportunities I get to meet with people and how many times they'll say, "Hey, that's interesting. Come back, we're interested." Cold calling is not for everyone, but it is one more marketing tool that you can be using to increase your sales.

GUARANTEED RESULTS

Competition How many of you have competitors? Oh, okay, almost everyone. I am glad to hear that. When you think of your competitor, open up your mind. It is too often that people say, "I sell widgets." Therefore, my competitor is the discount widget store down the street, the volume guy across the way; it's the person in the back of the catalog or magazine. If you are like most businesses you have many other competitors. Think about it. If someone is going out to buy a widget, are they saying, "I must have a widget" or are they saying, "I have discretionary income of $$$$ and I am going to purchase something." It may still be a widget; it may be a video widget. They may go by the CD department and find a CD changer that will go in their trunk, and they buy that instead. So, you can't be so narrowly focused that you say, "My competitor is only the person who directly competes in my kind of product or service." There are many areas that you compete in. So, when you think about those things, try to open up your mind so you are not limiting your efforts. If your business is renting cars you compete with all of the other rental places. You also compete with taxis and mass transportation. You may not have thought about it but if the people who rent your cars are families on vacation you also compete with all of the places they could spend their vacation money. That could include restaurants, resorts and attractions. Most people have a limited amount of money for vacation. If they spend more on lodging they have less for car rental.

Create Profitable Packages This is a gold mine! Everyone reading this book has heard this many times. But, they do not implement it. Group a

▼▼▼▼▼ GUARANTEED RESULTS ▼▼▼▼▼

series of products or services together. Put a special price on it and it's amazing what an incremental sales set-up it will be. Again, I mention I am part owner in a retail business. We do this every year with stocking stuffers. We put together a stocking with things other than our standard items. Then we include our retail products, and sell it at a special price. Many times people will like product packages because they can come in, plunk down plastic or write a check and be out the door - happy as could be and they do not have to bother with anything else. The package often will provide the person with a complete solution. "I don't need to buy all of these little items, I can buy this pre-packaged solution." You are happy because it's cash up front. It's immediate revenue and your cost is incurred much, much later. So, it has an excellent opportunity. Everyone can do it. I do not care what business you are in, you can develop some sort of packaging, some sort of combination, some sort of grouping that you can sell at a specialized price, still generate incremental sales and still generate increased profits. You can do it with baskets for any holiday. If you say my business is not like that, well you can still bundle products together. Look at all the software companies that now bundle a complete package of applications at one "low" price. Every business can bundle services and products to generate incremental sales and boost profits. Think about profitable packaging the next time you go to the car wash. They know that by packaging their services together they make it easier for the customer and they increase sales.

Create Urgency One of the most important goals in any marketing effort is creating a sense of urgency. For example, explain to your customer it's only available for two days

▼▼▼▼▼ GUARANTEED RESULTS ▼▼▼▼▼

or tell them there is only one available at this price. Urgency is the reason most coupons have expiration dates. If the coupon expires today I better use it. If your customer leaves your store or they leave your operation without a purchase, chances of them coming back have significantly decreased. I'm not saying they won't. But you need to give your customer a reason to purchase now. As opposed to your customer saying, "I am going to take this $250 and maybe I will buy it next month." Well, chances are that they are going to find a VCR or CD player or something else and that $250 will just disappears.

An important issue to address about urgency, once again, be honest. DO NOT make misleading claims to create urgency. If you have 100,000 widgets do not say you only have one left. All this does is cause trouble in the long run. It makes you and your company look bad. Create honest urgency.

Define Your Customer

You need to know your customer as well as you know yourself. Learn everything about them because the more you know, the easier it is to talk to them and the easier it is to have your people talk to them. You are in business to solve their problems. The better you know your customers the easier it will be to meet their needs and solve their problems. When you want to say something- you know their language. You know what they like; you know where they shop. If your customer shops at high-end stores, you want to treat them to a high-end experience. You do not want incongruency. You do not want them to come in and have someone standing at the counter popping their gum and saying, "What do you want?" The person may not immediately say "that's incongruent," but they will think it. The chance of them

▼▼▼▼▼ GUARANTEED RESULTS ▼▼▼▼▼

spending that $250 has just dropped off dramatically. Your business is based on the idea of providing a product or service that your customers want and need. If you do not truly know your customer how can you provide that service? Look at all the possible ways that you can to define your customer; e.g., age, gender, marital status, income, location, sales, etc. After all, the more you know the more you grow.

Develop A Charity Event Sponsoring or working with charity events are just some of the ways that you can be involved within your community; furthering exposure of your product or service, while helping you give back to your community. Work with, or join, a local service club. Consider Rotary or any of the other service clubs. They are a great way to meet people and help your community. Look for places that do not necessarily need your money but can use your expertise to help the organization. You can become the place to drop off canned food for the Salvation Army Food Drives. Your company can have the First Annual Halloween Food Drive for your community.

Develop A List Of Common Objections And How To Overcome Them If you know what the person is going to object to, you should immediately have an answer. How many of you have ever heard, "Your price is too high."? This is an excellent time to explain to the customer why your products are priced the way they are. "We provide extra services. We take extra care. We make sure that our work is guaranteed. We do these different things." Therefore, this price is justified. It

▼▼▼▼▼
GUARANTEED RESULTS
▼▼▼▼▼

does not always work, but at least they walk away saying, "Well, they are not just trying to gouge me." So always look at the objections that you are going to get. Price is going to be one of them. Hours are bad; location is bad; your work is bad; this is bad- I mean, objections are very common. Develop a list of how you're going to overcome them, how you're going to overcome them every time. This is an excellent tool for everyone you work with. Everyone needs to know what the potential customer is thinking and how to overcome the negatives. One of the best ways to do this is to answer the question before it is asked. For example if you know that your prices are higher than your competitions explain that up front to your customers. "Have you been looking at various widgets? As you look around you will find cheaper widgets. We are not the low price leader. We know that you want not only fair pricing but a well made widget. All of our widgets are made from only the finest materials, other companies use lower grade materials and don't provide the same guarantee that we do...." The sooner you develop the list of most common objections and how to overcome them, the sooner you will turn these objections into sales. This list makes you feel like you have the answers before you take the test. You are much more relaxed during the sales process because you have answers to the customers questions.

Develop a Marketing Budget

It's kind of like that sales person saying, "Well, I want my sales to go up kind of here." If you don't have a budget for your marketing--if you don't say, "This is what I'm going to spend and this is what my return is going to be", too many times you end up spending money foolishly, spending more than you wanted to spend and

▼▼▼▼▼
GUARANTEED RESULTS
▼▼▼▼▼

not reaching the outcome you desired. The other thing that happens and I see this all too often, is you put in $20,000 for marketing; "I spent $5,000 on a mailer and I only have one response, so I am not doing anything else." Well, you wasted that $5,000 because you are not doing anything to support it. Your budget should be based on results. One other important part about a marketing budget is it helps you to not waste money on all the ideas that walk in the door. "You need to buy the back cover of our magazine", or "We can have you on TV for only..." Develop your budget and stick to it.

Direct Mail When you send out a mailing, whether it is one letter or 100,000, you need to keep a few points in mind. The first point, if you are doing direct, is the envelope. You need to give people a reason to open it. When we do our mailings for Robinson & Associates, we make sure our stamps stand out. We select the most colorful, bright one we can find. Because it helps people to say, "Hey, that's different." Also on the envelope you should put a call to action. Give the reader a reason to open now! When you get a mailing from the magazine companies, like Publishers Clearing House, they always give you a reason to open the envelope. It will have something like, "You have won $10,000,000.00". That is a good way to get someone's attention. You can do the same by telling them what they will get from the information in the envelope.

When you send out correspondence, it's very easy to left and right justify--meaning everything looks great on both sides, like the pages in this book. When you get a personalized letter, does it look that way? No. When your mom or dad or friend or someone writes you, the first paragraph is indented, ragged on the right side. You want to do your letters that way--it looks more

▼▼▼▼▼ GUARANTEED RESULTS ▼▼▼▼▼

personal. It gets people to say, "This was not necessarily rattled off with a hundred thousand other ones on the same word processor." Indenting your paragraphs; makes it look more friendly. Also with computers you can include the person's name and company name throughout the letter. This also makes people feel more special. Most people love to hear or see their name. Include it a few times for added impact.

When you send a letter or any correspondence, the three most important parts are: <u>Headline</u> - this is the first part read. If it's a friendly letter, you do not have to put a headline, but it will not hurt. But if it's a solicitation of some sort, put on a headline: "Hey great news! We can save you money...." Try to make it benefit oriented: "Hey, we just received a new ... and it helps you by ...." Second most important part: <u>P.S.</u> How many of you get promotional mailings with all the stuff inside it and it always has a P.S.-- and you always read it? These aren't my studies. There are people who do research to see how people read their mail, and the P.S. is read almost 80% of the time. What you want the headline to do is educate and tell them, "Hey, this is what this letter is going to tell you." What you want the P.S. to do is say, "Hey, this is what the letter just told you." Third most important parts are the <u>Bullet Points</u> in between. Guess what? They are going to tell you again what you are trying to get across to the reader. Try to do four or five of them; make them bold and make them stand out; put subheadings. What you are trying to do is ensure that, if the person only reads the headline, they know that you have a "new ...." and the benefits to them are "---" that's not bad. If you could get that communicated to everyone you want- --you are head and shoulders above most people. Then, they are going to go to the P.S. if they read that far and they are going to see it again. You are still winning. And last,

▼▼▼▼▼ GUARANTEED RESULTS ▼▼▼▼▼

they're going to read the bullets. If they read all three, chances are they will read the entire letter. If they read only two of the things, the headline and the P.S., you have made your point. Direct mail is a science. Always try to improve your results by trying new words and new looks. You can improve your response simply by putting new messages on the outside of the mailer.

Direct Selling   Direct selling simply means how you work with a person one on one? You are doing it; your employees are doing it; other people at your business are doing it. Make sure that you have the best possible direct selling program that you can.

When you are doing direct selling always do more listening than talking. Ask your customers what they want, what they need and why. After you know this, it is very easy to apply the information to your product or service. For example; you manage a vacuum cleaner store and you sell vacuum cleaners. Too many times the sales person says, "Hello, may I help you!" So the customer is well trained and says, "Just looking!" That is the first mistake of the sales person. Just make conversation, comment on what they are wearing, or the weather. Now if the person says, "I am looking for a vacuum cleaner." You know that they are looking for the benefits that a vacuum cleaner gives them, i.e., cleaner carpets. At this point you need to stop selling and start listening. Ask what their needs are and then just listen to them. If they say, "I need one with enough power to clean up after my children and two dogs." Great now you have some information to make it easier for them to purchase. Now you can say, "With children and two dogs you need the Dirt King IV--it has enough power to get the dirt out of your carpet and it is still easy for anyone to use."

▼▼▼▼▼ GUARANTEED RESULTS ▼▼▼▼▼

You are not guessing at the problem they want solved, you are just answering the question that they have asked. The best way to sell is to listen to your customer's problem and then illustrate how your product or service solves it!

Also, test different ways to make the sale. Once you have developed the best way, make a script out of it and have all of your people use it until a better way is found.

Discounts You do not have to discount. Advertising and marketing people often say, "Well, cut the price. Tell them it's 30% off - people will come in then." You do not have to. I am not saying it's a bad idea, just that you do not have to do it. You can add value, and services and other products to make people perceive that there is a reason to purchase, other than just price. Discount one item - package another and people perceive that they are getting a lot for their money. Look at the way companies discount. Many times they package a group of products together and offer them at a discounted price. This allows them to keep their standard one item pricing and still offer a discount. For example; You group together a hamburger, drink and fries. Retail price $4.50 but as a group you sell it for $3.95. The customer does not get a lower price for just a hamburger. They get the discount only if they buy the special group. The restaurant increases their sales because the average customer only spends $3.00 per visit. Now you have increased some customers to $4.50. With enough sales, that can be the difference between a profit or loss for the business.

If you are only competing on price alone it is very hard to win. Always look for ways to add value. If you are going to discount, tell the customer what they are going to get, i.e., "Save $2,000". Test to see how people react. Is it better to say 50% or $2,000 savings. Test and see.

▼▼▼▼▼ GUARANTEED RESULTS ▼▼▼▼▼

Don't Just Follow Your Competition - Be A Leader

This happens all the time. At Widget World they say, "We will do an ad mailing and we will send out coupons, and we will have an offer of buy 2 get 1 Free." Next week, their competitor is doing the same offer. The week after that, another competitor is doing the same offer. Be different - be a leader. Try to do something that sets you apart. If you are number two or number three - you cannot win. Everyone is going to say, "Well, they did it first." So you lost on that account and you are in a price war. You are number two or three and you are trying to hold the tail of the dog. The leader is going to dictate the price because they have already told you that they would discount. Now, you are a discounter.

Look at what people in other industries do to increase sales or generate awareness. Try to look beyond your traditional ways of growing your business. If you work at a bank look at what fast food restaurants are doing. If you work for a fast food company look at what a clothing store in the mall is doing. Better yet look at what a company that goes after the same market but is in a different industry does. For example, if you go after families with young children look at what theme parks do, or clothing stores, or toy stores, etc. Think about any place that this family could be spending their money. You will get much better results if you do not just look at your competitors.

Drawings

You should have a fish bowl that says, "Put in your business card and win a "deluxe widget". The reason you want to do this is that you want your customer's name. Now

▼▼▼▼▼
GUARANTEED RESULTS
▼▼▼▼▼

that you have their name, you are going to send them information; you are going to educate them about the benefits of your products and services; you are going to ask them to purchase; and, you are going to ask them to come in. You want to know more about your customer. You want to know more things. You want to be able to get people who do not necessarily purchase, to give you information about themselves. For example; home phone number, are they married? So, again, think about your demographic model; You can make a more defined one every time because you get more information.

After the drawing is over take some time and publicize the winner. Put their picture up, send a story to your local media and make the most of the event.

Drop Box or Suggestion Box

Just have one. Suggestions are a great way to learn things that your customers want and that you can profit from. These are one of the most under-utilized marketing tools that all businesses have. These are the best ways to find out what your customers want. Think about it, why are you in business? To satisfy your customer's needs! What better way to find out about their needs than to ask them. This provides you with an open format for collecting information about the perception of your company and areas that your customers want changed. An important point to remember with a suggestion box is to use the suggestion and to acknowledge the comments. Send people a thank you or mention the idea the next time you see them. Also remember that the information that one customer gives you is only an indication. Ask other customers before you make any major changes.

▼
48

▼▼▼▼▼ GUARANTEED RESULTS ▼▼▼▼▼

Dropouts and Free Standing Inserts - FSI, Tip-Ins

These are exactly what the names say. They are inserted into other things and are made to drop out or to be free standing. You have all seen them and most of you have grumbled about them from time to time. When you get a magazine it has all of those subscription cards that fall out. You guessed it, those are drop outs. If the card stays in the publication they are called tip-ins. Once you get past all of those you get all the cards that make the pages open to them. The reason magazines use this technique is not because they want to frustrate you while you are trying to read your favorite articles, they do them because they are effective. You can do them in mailers or have FSIs put in your local news paper. This is only limited by your imagination. You could include a dropout in all of your invoices and statements that announces you now have a new product or service. Dropouts are effective because when it falls out people look at it when they pick it up.

Educate Your Employees

Educating your employees could be an entire book. In many businesses the employees are their first line of marketing. If you do not take the time to educate them on what to say, how to say it and when to say it, they will not say it the way you want them to. You need to invest time and energy into helping your employees to help your customers better than anyone else. You need to assume that your employees know very little. It is much better for you to be redundant than it is for you to skip areas that they need help. As I have said many times, everything your company does is marketing. That means that the better you educate your people, the easier it will be for them

▼

GUARANTEED RESULTS

to educate your customers and potential customers. Your education sessions can be very simple and do not need to take an entire day. An excellent way for people to learn is through role playing. Have all of your employees act as customers and see how they want to be treated and the information that they are looking for. Education is very often overlooked by companies because they assume that everyone knows what they should be saying and doing. This simply is not true. Educate your people. The more knowledgeable they are about your products, services, marketing and company philosophy the better they will help your customers.

Expect To Do More

One ad or one mailing to generate awareness will not work. You just can't do it one time. People are too busy. On average, people need to be exposed to your message seven or eight times before they are going to first recognize it. When you do your ad budget, when you do the marketing plan, plan to do your marketing efforts repetitively. If you say, "Well, I have enough money to run one ad"- take your spouse, friend, significant other to dinner, because all you are going to do is waste your hard earned money with one ad. Plan it effectively. Plan it efficiently. Say, "I know it's going to cost me $$$ to do it eight times and to write articles, so I'm going to have to do a smaller ad or I may have to stagger them." At least you are going to get the most from it that you can. Once is never enough, plan to hit prospects with a consistent message in a short period of time--seven or eight times.

Consistency is an important ingredient of any marketing effort's success. If you send seven letters to one person that all look different, that all say different things, you are going to have a minimal impact.

▼▼▼▼▼ GUARANTEED RESULTS ▼▼▼▼▼

Express Service — Make purchasing easy. Time is one of our most limited resources these days. We use cellular phones, pagers, faxes, voice mail, express mail, etc. - because we have to maximize our time. Your customers are the same way. Maximize the expediency with which they can do something. I do not mean rush them out of your business or rush them out of a meeting. Think about the number of times your customer could be purchasing from you but they think they do not have the time. There is a local hardware store within 1 mile of my home, but I go to the hardware store that is about 5 miles away because I know that they will have the product and serve me quickly. The one close to my home always has just one register open and if I need help in the store I cannot find anyone. It does not take any longer to ask a customer if they need anything else and to say "thank you"! That's how you generate incremental sales. You can provide expeditious service and you can still make the most from your sale.

Frequency Builder — A frequency builder tries to get a person in repeatedly--over and over and over again. Car washes are notorious for it. They give you a card that after it is stamped ten times the eleventh wash is FREE. They are building a habit. The better the habit they can build, the more likely the customers are to come back to them over and over and over. Set up the number. How many times do you have to get the person to drive up to your building, to come in and spend their money, before they say, "This is an easy place to get my widgets" If it's seven times- say after the seventh time, the eighth widget is free. Seven sets of new widgets, seven widgets serviced, you get the eighth one free.

▼▼▼▼▼ GUARANTEED RESULTS ▼▼▼▼▼

Whatever it needs to be to get that habit formed. Again, your marketing is going to be much more profitable, because they have developed a habit. They are in the habit of buying your products and services. You do not have to work as hard to pull them or push them in your door. When you choose a frequency builder decide the average number of times your customer purchases in a set time. If "your customer" normally purchases six widgets in six months you may make the card after seven the eighth is free. You have effectively increased their purchasing.

Important: This will work for all businesses. If I sold new cars I would tell customers that if they purchase four new cars from me in five years the next one is half price. If I were a Realtor I would tell people that, if you use me to buy three homes, the fourth one's commission to me will only be $100. This makes it easy for people to do more than the average.

Gift Certificates Many times people do not think about gift certificates. They do not think they work for the type of business that would offer gift certificates. Or, no one else in their industry uses them. If you are not using them you are truly missing a great opportunity. The first thing about gift certificates that I like is that they generate immediate revenue. A person gives you $20 for a gift certificate and you have no expense. Or only the expense of printing it. And, many times, they do not even redeem it. This makes them very profitable and generates awareness for your company. Your gift certificates can be done very simply. You can buy pre-printed certificates or you can just use a laser printer and print your own custom gift certificates on a nice quality paper. The most important part about gift certificates is that you tell people they are available. Make signs that tell people why they should buy your

▼▼▼▼▼ GUARANTEED RESULTS ▼▼▼▼▼

gift certificates and how they can. List the benefits of them; perfect for birthdays, anniversaries, never the wrong size or color, easier to mail, never out of stock, etc. Any company can use gift certificates. People say, "Our products are business to business not retail. How could we do gift certificates?" Have one business buy them for another. Many of my business clients would love a gift certificate to a computer store or an office supply business. All you need to be is a little bit creative and you will be amazed at all the ideas you can come up with for gift certificates.

Gift Ideas Throughout Your Business

Here's another one that's just too easy not to do and that is make everything a gift. Make everything fun. Humans are the worst at, "I do not like to buy gifts." If someone says, "This is a perfect gift." Hey, that's all I need, a perfect gift. That's what I was shopping for. So package products and services so they are gifts: it's a natural, easy purchase. As I mentioned earlier, people want to be led. Gift ideas make it easy for those of us with busy schedules that do not get out enough. This is a good reason to do signs and banners. Use them to educate your customers about all of your gift opportunities.

Going To Trade Shows Or Being In A Trade Show

When you go to a trade show or are in a trade show have a set purpose. A significant amount of time and money is spent on a trade show. If you are going to make the investment, you should have a very well defined outcome. You should also very carefully plan who you want to see and who you want

▼▼▼▼▼ GUARANTEED RESULTS ▼▼▼▼▼

to make sure sees you. You need to plan and practice what everyone is going to say at the show. Having scripts is very important. Many times when you are at a show you are introducing a new product or service. It is vital for your success at the show to make sure that everyone knows the benefits of your products and services. It never fails that your largest potential client always talks with the least knowledgeable person in your company. By having a pre-trade show meeting, you can help to make sure that everyone in the company is well prepared to achieve your pre-defined goals. Trade shows are a great opportunity for most companies if you prepare for them. One important part of the preparation is your advertising and handout materials. If you are going to participate in a show, maximize your impact with advertising in the trade publications that will help you to stand out from your competition. Also you need to have strong marketing materials. The people you see are going to be deluged with messages--yours must stand out from the masses. Plan ahead for your ads and the trade show materials. You will be very happy you did and your show will be more successful.

Guarantee Every company should have an unconditional guarantee. If your products and services do what you say they will do you should offer a complete guarantee. Now that we have that out of the way let's talk about your guarantee for a moment.

You need to use this as one of your marketing tools. Many companies have great marketing tools but they never tell anyone about their guarantee. In Marketing 101 you learn that when a person makes a purchase they are taking a risk. They are spending

▼▼▼▼▼ GUARANTEED RESULTS ▼▼▼▼▼

money on an unknown. Many companies will put the Good Housekeeping seal of approval on their product to help reduce that risk. Your customers will think, "If it is good enough for Good Housekeeping, it is good enough for me." Well, you should be doing that now with your guarantee. If your widgets will help save a person money, tell them how much they will save and then show them your guarantee. By doing this you have reduced their risk to almost nothing. If your widget does not work, they get their money back. What could be better for both of you. The guarantee will get them to try your product or service and they no longer have to take all the risk. After this I am always asked, "What if I get people wanting their money back?" If your product or service does what you say it will you have nothing to worry about. You only have to worry if it doesn't.

Have fun — Try to have all your people have fun. Make your business fun. Sounds kind of silly? If you are not having fun, why are you doing it? I love what I do. I am fortunate. I love helping people with their marketing and I like seeing businesses succeed. You have to be the same way. The more you like what you do, the happier you are and the more fun you have, the more likely people are to say, "I want to come in and experience that again. I want to enjoy myself, because I had fun." That makes it really easy for people to come back repeatedly. This is just simple logic. Who wants to do business with people that are not having fun? Your customers are people and they have a need that they want someone to fill. If you make it fun, it's easier to do business with you!

▼▼▼▼▼ GUARANTEED RESULTS ▼▼▼▼▼

Have Your Own Trade Show

You may be thinking, "I'm just a little widget maker. I can't have a trade show." I am sorry to tell you, but you are wrong. Anyone can have a trade show. You can make it as small as you want it to be. You can use complementary products or services and bring them into your location. It gives you an opportunity to bring in four or five different complementary businesses who may have customers that have not experienced your service or seen your facilities. It gives you a chance to all work together for a common good. You do not have to charge them an exorbitant fee, you can promote it together, you can work together and you can end up having a really good show on a smaller scale. You do not have to call it a trade show. You can call it anything you want to call it. Maybe you want to say that it is a Fair, New Product Show or an Expo. But, basically that's what it comes down to--it's a trade show. It is an opportunity to show people what you do, who you are, new products or just an opportunity to say hello and thank you to your customers.

If You Build A Better Mouse Trap They Will Beat A Path To Your Door. This is a LIE

Having a great product or service is not enough. Many companies with great products and services go out of business every year. You need to have a product or service that people need and they need to know that it exists. If people do not know about your product they can't purchase it. Always plan to market your product or service. You may only need to run classified ads, or send out an occasional press release, but you are always going to need to do some marketing. It is also

▼▼▼▼▼ GUARANTEED RESULTS ▼▼▼▼▼

important to remember that you will also have competitors. As they start to grow they will start to take away some of your customers. Please remember that if you are in business to build a better widget, that is wonderful, but most companies are in business to build a great widget and to SELL them.

Incentives-Internal and External

Rewards are a great way to increase sales, customer satisfaction and increase your chances of success. Give your sales force and your customer service department a reason to do their job a little better. One of the best reasons is money. It does not have to be lots of money. It does not have to necessarily be money. It could be; days off, a prize or even a gift certificate. The first person who sells ten widgets gets a half day vacation. Programs like this work if everyone plays the game. Most of the time we look at marketing and incentives in terms of the external world. Buy 10 widgets--get the eleventh one free. You need to do the same type of thing internally. Give your employees a reason to excel. Too many times, people think it's okay to be just mediocre. Give them an advantage; give them a reason to go above and beyond the every day. People like to be challenged. Give your staff a reason to be better customer service people. A program that we use with some of our clients is the "Mystery Person". We have an unknown person listen for the mystery tag line. For example; Widget world wants more people to know that we now service widgets. We do our mystery program and every time the mystery person hears someone say, "Did you know we also service widgets" the mystery person makes note of it. At the end of the day the mystery person goes around and gives a dollar to everyone that they heard say the mystery tag line.

▼▼▼▼▼ GUARANTEED RESULTS ▼▼▼▼▼

Programs like these are fun and rewarding for the employees and for Widget World.

Incremental Sales Whenever I think of incremental sales, I think of McDonalds. They are one of the best companies that I know of for generating incremental sales. How often have you purchased food at McDonalds and heard, "Would you like fries with that?", or "Would you like to try a hot apple pie?", or "Would you like orange juice with your breakfast?" That is how they generate incremental sales. Incremental sales very simply means increasing your customer's average order. Incremental sales very often will mean the difference between struggling to get by and being profitable! What would a 5% or 10% increase in sales do for your bottom line? Incremental sales are an excellent way to do profitable marketing. When the person walks in, you have to think, "They're coming in to buy a widget. What other products or service do they need to get the most satisfaction out of the widget?" If you do not like the idea of incremental sales, think of it as customer service. Nothing makes someone more upset then when they buy the new widget, they get home, and then find out it needed batteries or it needed a this or it needed a that. You should automatically be putting it all together as a package. Have the product, have the batteries, have the extended warranty, have the case, have it all ready for them. Then when they purchase, you did not just get the $250 sale, you got the $350 sale. The second $100 is very, very profitable because it is straight incremental business. It's just a matter of thinking about what the customer wants and needs. You have to think for them. I bought a VCR recently. I said, "Is everything I need in here?" They said, "Yes." It did not have the right cable. So, now I am not happy

▼▼▼▼▼ GUARANTEED RESULTS ▼▼▼▼▼

with the place that I purchased it from and they could have gotten the incremental sale and a happy customer as opposed to no incremental sale and a former customer who does not like them very much right now.

If you are doing photo processing, when you process one roll of film, guess what? The customer needs another! When a customer drops off film it is time to buy more. If they are picking up their prints it is time to buy more film or drop off more film or maybe get new "fresh" batteries for their camera. Think about these things and always be working towards generating incremental sales. It takes high repetition to generate awareness...seven or eight times minimum. Notice I have mentioned that about three times now?

Joint or Cross Promotion

Figure out someone you can work together with and promote each other's business. Look for a non-competing company that has similar or complementary clients, similar type services, similar type quality and do a joint or cross promotion. Joint and cross promotions work very, very well. They help new customers to learn about your products and services and they help your customers to find other businesses that they will like working with. "Cross promotion" means: I have a portrait studio; you have a frame shop - I recommend that everyone purchase their frames from you; you recommend that everyone has their portrait done at my studio. We promote back and forth. "Joint" means: We do something together. Here's a package of an 8x10 and a frame. You bought one from him and one from me - it normally would have cost you $50, but since we are promoting jointly, it's going to cost you $35. They get increased awareness; we get awareness. Both companies get

▼▼▼▼▼
GUARANTEED RESULTS
▼▼▼▼▼

increased sales and more people learn about your increased business. Everyone wins.

Joint Venturing Joint ventures give you the opportunity to increase your exposure and reduce your cost. Joint venture simply means working with some other company. It could be on a promotion, on service or on service after the sale. One of the first places you should look for joint venturing opportunities is with your suppliers. Many times they would like you to more heavily promote and sell their products or services. You see joint promotions all the time. When your local grocery store has a sale on Nestle candy bars they are joint promoting with Nestle. Nestle approached the store, or the store approached Nestle and said, "We want to promote the sale of your candy. What can we do?" Next an offer is developed which includes how and what will be promoted. Nestle sees this as a great way for them to increase sales. The grocery store will increase sales and have increased traffic and hopefully will have increased purchases of other products. Joint ventures are an excellent way to develop a win-win situation. You may be surprised at the number of people who would like to joint venture with you. Many times a company that supports you or that you support would like to joint venture. At Widget World they may do a joint venture with the Widget Financing Company. Both companies know that the more widgets that are sold the more they both benefit. One important point to remember about joint venture is you need to develop it just like any other marketing effort. You need to set attainable goals. When it is going to start, when it is going to end, and who is responsible for all the work that needs to be done.

GUARANTEED RESULTS

Know What Your Customers Like and Dislike

I have repeated this many times, but the more you know about your customers, the more effective your marketing and advertising will be. A discount or dollars off or free this and free that is not always what they want. Many times, they may just want longer hours. I run my own business - my hours are always long. Nothing irritates me more than not to be able to do something that I need to get done, like drop off a bank deposit. Well, they close at 5:00. I may pay a little bit more, but if the bank is open until 8:00 PM then I am going to change banks. So, think about what your customer's likes and dislikes are and provide accordingly.

Let everyone in your company know that all of your paychecks come from the customer. Something that is very important is continuing the education that you are getting now with the people you work with and the people that work for you. Many times we know this information. You know this information. You must educate your people, the people who are actually meeting with the customer. Otherwise it does not get done. You have to work very hard to make your customers and your employees understand what you are doing. You will have a weak link in the company chain if anyone in the company does not understand what the customer wants. Remember, your company is only as strong as its weakest link.

Licensing

Licensing is a very profitable program for all businesses. With licensing you sell a license for the use of your product or services name or way of doing business. This is an excellent way to generate revenue for your company

▼▼▼▼▼
GUARANTEED RESULTS
▼▼▼▼▼

without selling off the business. For example; you know how to make widgets that help people stay cool. Your company currently is selling your widgets in California. You know that people in Florida would love this product. You contact a company or person in Florida who says, "I want to sell these in Florida." You sell them the license for the right to sell them in that state. They may pay you a fee for the initial licensing. Now every time they buy more of your cool widgets you both make money. You benefited by generating the up front licensing revenue, which also increased your sales, and now people in more areas are hearing about your product. If you do want to license your products or services I recommend that you contact your lawyer. This is too important to be left to chance. The wording of the license may mean you make or lose millions. If you want more information about the subject either look in your local libraries or book stores. Licensing can be an excellent way to generate immediate revenue and to increase your sales.

Lifetime Value of Customers

"LTV" -- Lifetime value means: How much is that person worth to your business over time? Today they may buy one widget or new batteries. But over the next three years, five years, seven years - what is that worth to your business? The next time they may buy your top of the line widget package. They may buy whatever you have to sell at the top of the line. So, think of a lifetime value. People tend to get very short-sighted and say, "I did a mailer; they came in and bought batteries--the mailer did not work." They came in--it's a good sign; they bought batteries--not a great sale; but, hey, can I get them in again? Is there an opportunity for them to come back? And now, the lifetime value idea starts and it becomes: "Yes, I spent $500 on a

▼▼▼▼▼
GUARANTEED RESULTS
▼▼▼▼▼

mailer, but they have been in over and over and now they have spent $1,000 to $3,000--and that's well worth the money."

Local Personalities or Celebrities to Visit

People are infatuated with celebrities. They do not have to be world famous or on Lifestyles of the Rich and Famous. They need to be people that your customers would like to meet, say "Hi" to, or just get an autograph from. Every city has them. It does not have to be Michael Jordan if you are in Chicago or Lee Iococca if you are in Detroit. There are many people that your customers would like to meet. It can be a local radio or television personality, your mayor or governor, local professional athletes or coaches, authors, business people, anyone that your customer would like to see, perhaps someone who is a specialist in your industry. Much of the time, the personality that you would like to work with uses your products or services. Just say, "Hey, could I have you come in on a Saturday for two hours and I will provide your next ten widgets free." Because they are already around, it can be very easy for them to do and if they already like your widgets why not ask. It is important to mention some personalities will not do "visits". If your first choice says, "No" call your second choice. This is another great way to generate awareness and excitement, so that people will want to come to your place of business.

Make Good Customer Service a Priority

I keep mentioning customer service, but if you make customer service a priority, some of your marketing woes are going to take care of

GUARANTEED RESULTS

themselves. Your customers are going to want to come back and they are going to enjoy their experience. That means your marketing does not have to work quite as hard. The best way to provide good customer service is to first know what your customers want. Too many times people work very hard at providing great customer service but it is not the service that the customer wants. For your customer service to be an asset, everyone needs to provide the same exceptionally high level of service. All the people that are in contact with your customers and prospective customers need to understand the importance of customer service. For example; many times people forget that accounts receivable is a part of customer service. (You need to make that a part of customer service as well.) Often times if an accounts receivable matter is handled professionally you will retain that customer. That means one less new customer that you need to develop.

Make Your Message Consistent

If you see me Monday through Thursday on a business day, I will be wearing a dark suit, white shirt and fun tie - every day. Friday is casual day. I work with a number of high-tech clients and that's the way they are, so that is the way I am. But, it's consistent. They know exactly how I will be when I show up. And the thing that's strong about that is they know what to expect, they know what they are going to get. If your client gets great customer service one day and the next day they get terrible service they are not coming back, because they do not know what to expect. You can give them bad treatment every time and, as long as they know they are going to get bad treatment, a lot of times they are forgiving. People's decisions do not always make sense. If you have a great product but, you do not have great service

▼▼▼▼▼
GUARANTEED RESULTS
▼▼▼▼▼

or you have a great product and a great price, but you give them awful service, it may not bother them because they know what to expect every time. How many times have you heard someone say: "Go to So-n-So...they are a little rough around the edges, but they do great work." It's the inconsistency that we can't handle. And you need to be consistent in everything you do: look, feel, touch, smell, everything--consistency.

One of my clients works with high-end clients and he asked me, "Does our restroom need to be clean?" I said, "Do your clients use the restroom?" He said, "Yes". I thought, "What have I been doing here? Of course it does." That's part of the consistency of experience. When you go to McDonalds, they do not tell you this is going to be a five star restaurant with linen napkins and crystal goblets. They tell you it's going to be quick, fair priced and it's going to be clean from front to back. We have gotten in the habit that we accept that and we say, "That's excellent." You need to look at your business the exact same way. If there is gum stuck to the floor and the counter is dirty and the person's fingernails are dirty, I guarantee you, I am going to think that your widgets are bad. They could be the best ones I have ever gotten. But, everything else around me told me that you do not care! They did not pay attention to details! So be consistent. This is doubly true for your marketing efforts--develop a good clean look and stay with it.

Make Your Products Festive

One simple way to increase sales is to make your product or service stand out; make it pop; use bright colors that your customers will react to. The reason you need to do this is because your customers are being

▼

GUARANTEED RESULTS

bombarded with marketing messages every day. Whether it's people trying to shake your customers hand, balloons, streamers or flashing lights, you need to do something to stand out and make it easy for people to notice your products or services. You need to merchandise. You need to make your products and services stand out. Put a bow on it; put a ribbon on it; put something that moves when the air conditioner comes on. Any of those things make it that much easier for someone to say, "What is that?" This should be music to your ears! You need to think what a great thing to hear, "What is that?" Because now you have an open opportunity to sell. They have just said, "I am interested; tell me why I need one of those." That's what it comes down to. If you can get people to say, "Tell me about this product or service", you are more than half way to reaching the sale. Next, you want to use your sales script that walks the customer through the benefits of your product or service and then you will be ready to make the cash register ring. Remember you are in business to meet your customer's needs-- being festive and happy helps to set you apart and better satisfy their needs.

Make Promotions and Sales Prominent

If you are going to have a promotion or sale, make it so everyone that might like to know about it does. Too many companies hide that they are having a sale. They have an entire area of sale items and it has the word "SALE" in one inch block letters above it. Well, nobody knows it's on sale. You want to sell these products, right! Well, the best way to do that is to tell people, not to hide the fact. I agree with the retail strategy where sale items are located in the back of the store, so that people have to walk through the entire store to find it-

▼▼▼▼▼ GUARANTEED RESULTS ▼▼▼▼▼

that's fine. But tell people. Don't be embarrassed about it. Say it's fifty percent off. That's what people are looking for. Get them interested, do not hide it. If you have a promotion - make it the biggest and best promotion you can make. I was talking with a friend who was doing a movie preview. The preview was so successful that they had more people show up than the theater could hold. The theater manager turned people away. Why wouldn't you let them in to see some other movie and make money on the concessions that they will buy while they are there? You need to keep this in mind when you have a sale. Sure they are buying the sale items at a discount but what about the other items they are purchasing? This all adds to your profits!

Make the Customer Your Number One Priority

This book is entitled *Guaranteed Results*. The reason I chose this title is that it is written to improve many areas of your business. It is about making your business a success. The best way to do this is by making your customers the most important part of your business. If you look at everything that your company does or can do from your customers perspective your business will improve. Make everyone in your company a customer service specialist. It does not matter what they do on a day-to-day basis. All that matters is that they know that the most important person in any company is the customer. Develop programs that will make your customers feel special. Have a Customer Appreciation Day or Week. (Everyday should be!) Give them a chance to meet the president or manager. Most customers think that it is very special to meet the executives in a company. Always look for ways that you

GUARANTEED RESULTS

can say "Thank you". After all, if it was not for your customers you would not have a business!

Media/Public Relations

Many people ask me, "How do we do public relations. You know, that FREE advertising." First there is no such thing as a free lunch or free advertising. Public relations is telling the media about newsworthy events that are happening with your company. You can include such items as new product introductions, new employees, new ways of doing business, new clients, new services, announcements of technological breakthroughs, announcements of honors or awards, etc. All of these are examples of times when you want to do press releases. The media is interested in these types of business happenings because they are news. In your announcements you should include who, what, when, where, why and how. Always make it newsworthy. People that have worked in the media will tell you over and over again. Make it news, do not make it sales. Yes, it can have some sell in it, but the number one priority is that it's newsworthy. A trade show is newsworthy. As long as you are talking about it so people learn something and people look at it and say, "Hey, that was newsworthy."

You also need to develop a comprehensive list of the "right" people to get your information to. You want the editors, writers, producers and reporters that are most likely to see your information as news to get a copy of your news release. If you sell automobiles do not send your releases to the editor of the garden section. Take some time and get the names and addresses of the people that want this information. You can usually call the publication or just look in the front of most magazines and newspapers. The other point that is very important is to continually update the

GUARANTEED RESULTS

information. People change jobs fairly often and they want information to be sent to their attention, not their predecessor. Also make sure you know the proper spelling of their name and their title. You are asking them for help, so you want to make a good impression and having the correct contact information shows that you cared enough to be professional and accurate. When you do get a mention or an article it never hurts to send the writer or editor a thank you note.

Networking It's getting out and meeting people and educating them about what you do. You may choose to network on the golf course or at your children's school functions. You may also choose to join a leads group or a networking group. All of these networking ways are only as good as you make them. In a networking group you meet on a regular basis and everyone in the group is in a non-competing business. That means your group may have a banker, lawyer, accountant, plumber and an electrician. It will never have two plumbers. The most important part about networking is educating the other members about what a good lead is for you. The better you educate the people in your group the better leads you will get. As always you need to educate them about the benefits of your product or service and you need to tell them what you are looking for. Networking can be extremely profitable for many businesses. If you are thinking about networking, ask business associates and friends if they belong to a group. Most groups allow you to visit a couple of times before you join. Visit different groups to see in which group you feel most comfortable with. The more you like it the more you will put into the group and the better your results will be.

▼▼▼▼▼
GUARANTEED RESULTS
▼▼▼▼▼

New Products/Service Introductions

Always have them. This is a great excuse for people to come see you and your company and hear your name. You should spend most of your marketing time giving people an excuse to give you a call or stop by. Whenever you or your company adds a significant new product or new piece of equipment, send out the release. "Widget World now has a new state of the art widget maker that gives you better quality widgets in less time." (Notice that I always stress the benefits to the consumer.) Again, it gives people an excuse to come in; and a reason to say, "Hey, I should go see what that thing will do." The same media release should also be sent out to all of your current customers and good prospects. Just make copies of the press release and say, "Hey Betty, wanted you to know that we have this. Hope to see you in here soon." Or you can use this as an excuse to call them or have an open house. The most important rule to remember when you do an introduction is "make it informative and have fun!"

Newsletter

Newsletters are a great way for you to get your information to the customer. Make it informative and use it as a sales tool. Start out by deciding who you want to read it and what you want them to get from it. After you have done this, you can select the best ideas for columns or articles in each issue. Keep in mind that many companies do many different newsletters, one for the staff, one for sales people, one for new customers, one for each different product. After you know who you want to read it and what is going to be in it, start thinking about how it will look. It does not have to be fancy, but

▼▼▼▼▼ GUARANTEED RESULTS ▼▼▼▼▼

it needs to positively reflect on you and your company. Visit your local quick printer or photocopy center. They can tell you what they will charge to print them. Then you need to develop the page layout, if you cannot do it yourself, you can also ask the printer or look at some of your local designers. (IMPORTANT- You need to shop for the best value. Value = Price + Quality + Service. The prices that you are quoted can vary greatly. Get at least three estimates from each of the different people that will work on the newsletter with you.) There are many places that can do the design and printing for you. The one thing that makes doing a newsletter difficult is, doing it consistently. Do not say you are going to send one out every month, because most likely you will not. It takes too much time and too much effort - you get behind on it and then do not do it at all. Consider semi-annual or quarterly distribution. Let the amount and nature of your information drive the frequency of your communications to your customers. The newsletter only works if you do it. One last thing to think about is have a few people that will help you with it. You will always need articles and help with getting it done. Having help on a newsletter is a necessity!

On-hold Messages On-hold messages are a great customer service and sales tool. Most phone systems can have a tape player connected to them that allows you to play a pre-recorded message. You want to make the message benefit rich to your customer, and make it simple. This is one more way for you to advertise products or services that you have to offer. Think of this as a soft sell ad. You want to tell them what they get, the benefit, and what you want them to do. This also gives you an opportunity to say thank you and to tell them that you care about them. This

▼▼▼▼▼
GUARANTEED RESULTS
▼▼▼▼▼

is another good place to have fun. Make the message enjoyable for your customer. You can do your message very simply, just by saying, "We have a new product or we have a new service that you should ask us about." This gives you the opportunity to create awareness, create a reason for them to do something different.

Open Displays   For those of you that have retail outlets, make it easy; make it open; make it simple for people to get around. Do not shove everything together so it's a battle. Make it easy for your customer to spend time in your facilities. People want to look at what they are buying. They also want room to move around. Think about your customer for a minute. If they are new mothers, what do they need your displays to be like. Let's think about this a minute. The first point that comes to my mind is that they need enough room to push a stroller through the area. This is just one simple point but it illustrates how important the layout of your display area is. Many times if your displays are too close together the new mother will not come in because she does not have room for the stroller. That means lost revenue for you! People want to touch and feel what they are buying, give them room to comfortably do that.

Open House   Hold an Open House. Everyone has special machines or areas that people and your customers want to see. An open house is a good time for you to educate your customers about products or services that they are not currently purchasing. This is also a good time to help them understand your pricing. If you can show them with equipment, technology and time how your widget is made, many times that helps them to understand the

GUARANTEED RESULTS

reasons you charge the price you do. Set things up, show people around. People are always interested. If a person says "No, I don't have time now," set a time to have him come back. Show your customers the different things you do. You will be amazed at how much rapport you develop and how much more likely they are to come back and use your different services or say, "I didn't know you could..." Have an open house. The most important part from your perspective is to make the Open House convenient for your customers. If your customers work 9-5, do not make your Open House from 3-5. Consider holding it on Saturday or in the evening when your customers are available.

Parade of Products and Services

Develop twenty things that people should know they can buy at your store and display them. Restaurants do it all the time with their daily specials. You should always have a parade of products. These may be your ideas of what your customers need now. If you are in a business that has different products for different seasons, list the products that people will need for the next season. You can also do this for upcoming holidays or events. This is a good reminder to have around the company. You could put this information on a fax form and send it weekly to all of your customers and prospects. The parade of items can also be effective as an internal program. Develop the top twenty items that you want your sales people to mention over the next week, month or quarter. You may want to mention some new products as well as some products that need a little boost in sales.

▼▼▼▼▼ GUARANTEED RESULTS ▼▼▼▼▼

Phone-In Contests Contact some of your local radio stations and tell them you will provide widgets for them to give away to callers that guess the weight of a widget or the answer to a widget trivia question. Make it fun and make it something that your customers will be interested in. Try to be on the stations that most of your customers listen to. Radio stations will give anything away. Some of you that are in larger markets like Chicago, New York, L.A., may not be able to accomplish this on one of the major stations, but you normally can get a secondary station who will say, "Sure, I'll give away widgets for you." You can even have them call your number.....now they know your phone number, too! Not bad! If they can call you, we have them that much closer to saying, "I really liked that widget. I'm going to go back there." You have also increased awareness and hopefully have reminded a few people that they need widgets today.

Plan What You Expect The Return To Be From Your Marketing Investment Now we are going to be accountants. All the marketing you do has to have a return on investment. If it does not, it's wasted money. Fortunately, our economy is growing, but it has not grown enough that we can all just sit around and waste money. Sit down and say, I am going to do a newsletter; it's going to cost me $250 a quarter, and from that $250 investment, I need to see $5,000 in sales. Track the results. Too many times we lose sight of the fact that the only reason we use these marketing tools is to increase sales. Your marketing needs to provide a return on investment. Remember, you increase sales by educating your customers on how your

▼▼▼▼▼
GUARANTEED RESULTS
▼▼▼▼▼

widgets help solve their problems. One other way to look at this is to only say that you will pay for results. If the marketing does not provide results you have no reason to do it. One important point to mention is you need to give the program enough time to see the results. It takes time for people to see your marketing effort and to react. You cannot rush greatness.

Price Everyone comments that price is an important concern. In a study that was done by US. News and World Report, price ranked eighth out of ten in buying decisions. So, when everyone calls in and says, "What's your price," and they go to the cheapest place, it's because they do not know a better way to find out why they should purchase from you. The survey found that quality and service were the two most important reasons why people buy. Look at the companies that very seldom talk about price. Take Mercedes for example. Their entire business is based on quality and service. When was the last time you heard Mercedes having a tent sale or "we'll pay $3,000 for any trade in." They always stress quality and service. That is what separates them from all the others. So, if you are worried about the competitor that is offering a coupon that is ten cents lower than yours, find a way to show that your quality and service is better than theirs. It is very difficult to win on price alone. If all you compete on is price you are going to need to do an extremely high volume and always be looking for ways to cut costs. Educate your customers about the facts that price is not the most important part of purchasing your product or service. One last point about price is that you can sometimes show a higher initial price but an increased savings over time. For example; Water heater A- price $300, Water heater B- price $400. Same size, same company, same guarantee, same service, same

▼▼▼▼▼
GUARANTEED RESULTS
▼▼▼▼▼

quality. But Water heater B is twice as energy efficient. For the customer, that means a savings of over $1,000 during the average life of the water heater. The most important point for you to remember about price is that you need to educate your consumers about what makes your widgets a better value. Not just cheaper!

Provide A List Of Best Or Most Popular Items To Buy

People always want to buy what everyone else is buying. So, tell them. When someone comes into your facility, have a list or a sign that says, "Here is the most popular widget. Here's the most popular service. The #4 is the most popular sandwich. Here's the most popular package from our photo processing lab." So that the people have a reason to say, "Well, yes I can do that." People basically follow the pack--they like to follow the trends of everyone else. So, tell them. Books sell millions of copies by being listed on the "Best Seller" list. People want to know that other people thought that this particular product or service had merit.

Public Speaking Engagements

How many of you in your community have Rotary, Kiwanis, Lions, Optimists, Lady's Auxiliaries, flower clubs, pet clubs, any of these organizations? Most of them have or need new widgets or widgets repaired. Most of them need to know a better way of using their widgets. They want to know about advancements in widgets. Teach them. You know all about your products and services as well as trends in the industry. All you have to do is put it in a simple easy to follow format and explain it to them. It's not that hard. You know the information - you talk

▼▼▼▼▼ GUARANTEED RESULTS ▼▼▼▼▼

about your products and services every day. Now you are doing it for a small group. All you have to do is go talk about it. Hopefully, you have an opportunity to get fifty or twenty-five or eight new people who know about the products and services that you provide. It does not have to be long. Most speaking engagements last about fifteen minutes. Take some samples and you can hide behind those for seven of the fifteen minutes. It goes pretty quick, and you will be amazed, you can get some very, very good results. Try to start out with some smaller local groups and work your way up to larger groups.

Putting Your Sales Messages On Everything

It is very hard to give your customers too much information. You should look at everything you do and see if that is a good place for your advertising message. Look at your invoices, sales receipts, business cards, merchandise tags, etc. Whenever you have something printed for your company, see if you can include a simple sales message. It will not cost you any more for this and you get one more avenue to provide your customer with information. A great example of this is seen in the banking industry. Most banks do not just give you a receipt when you make a transaction, they also have on the top or the bottom a sales message. They may tell you about a new service or their CD rate. You can do the same for your company. Look at the different forms you use and the different tools you provide to your clients. Usually all of these could include a sales or customer service message.

Radio Ads

Thirty or sixty seconds is what you normally buy in radio air time. It's not

▼▼▼▼▼ GUARANTEED RESULTS ▼▼▼▼▼

very much time. You know your customers so well that in thirty seconds you can get across the benefits two or three times....in two or three different ways. Make it enjoyable, make it fun; make it stand out. You do not want the announcer just doing the reading, because they hear that all day long and they are just going to tune it out. So, do whatever you can to make it fun. This is going to be a thirty or sixty second sales presentation. Think about the problems that your customers want solved and tell them about your solution and why they want to use you over anyone else.

Buying the radio time. If you have never bought radio time you may want to talk with either an ad agency or a media buying service. Both of them will buy the media for you. The media buying service only buys media. They usually charge a little less but that is all they do. I would say the best thing for you to do is to talk with a few of each and see who you feel the most comfortable with. Whether you use a service or you do it yourself you always want to keep in mind that all you care about is the most cost effective way to reach your customers - not the universe. Always look at the cost per thousand (CPM) for your target. The radio station should be able to provide you with this information. You need to tell them who your target is and they can tell you the rest. Also listen to the station and call a few of the advertisers and ask them how the station is working for them. You need to invest enough that you can generate a consistent message and be repetitive. Media buying can be complex. If media buying is new to you, work with a professional for a while. You will save money in the long run.

▼▼▼▼▼ GUARANTEED RESULTS ▼▼▼▼▼

Remember, It's Five Times More Expensive To Get A New Customer Than It Is To Keep A Current One

It's kind of staggering because I have people who say, "Wow, I have all these customers who have used us once." Well, let's get them to use us twice, three and four times. Because, again, getting back to the idea of profitable marketing, that's one of the keys. It is much cheaper to get them back in the door over and over than it is to get new customers in for the first time. This is all part of the idea--that you want your customers to have a great experience when they purchase from you so they will come back. How many times do you follow-up after the sale to make sure they are happy? Do you send a thank you note? Do you ask if you can be of more service? Do you remind them that it is time to purchase again? These are all ways of showing your customers that you care and that you want their business. People like to feel needed. They want to know they are an important part of your business.

Remember That Everything Your Company Does Affects Your Marketing

You are going to put down this book and start thinking about your business and what you do in a new light. You are going to look at it from a marketing driven standpoint. You now realize that everything your company does affects your marketing. As you look at each area or part of your business, think, "That's a part of my marketing now. How does it help me help my customers? What is my customer going to get from this product or from me carrying this line; from me selling this." That's the way you have to look

▼▼▼▼▼ GUARANTEED RESULTS ▼▼▼▼▼

at it, because that's a part of your marketing. Everything you do affects your marketing. Remember that people buy benefits or solutions...not features. I see this all too often. We have a new widget maker with this type of system and it uses this type of chemicals. The customer does not care about any of that. What the customer cares about is that the quality is going to be unmatched; the color of the widget won't fade; that the widget for Aunt So-n-So is going to come out the best it possibly can. So, always think of it from a benefits perspective. It's a silly thing, but it's important: You never get a second chance to make a first impression. Always work with the people to make that first impression memorable. And, hopefully, it's memorable in a positive way. Talk to them; get to know them; make them family. So they say, "I had a great experience. I want to come back in again. I want to experience that again." Because that's going to help you again, get that incremental sale that saves you from having to get new customers all of the time.

Radio Remote Broadcasts

Radio stations will come out to your location, set up their van, set up whatever fun stuff they have, draw traffic, create awareness, get people to try you--it's a good idea. It can be very, very effective. It can be done very cost effectively and it can get new people to say, "Hey, I should go by there." The station will bring along T-shirts, hats and plenty of fun stuff. And that makes it that much easier for someone to say "I really want to go there. I want to take the time out of my busy day to go and experience this new place." This is a good way for customers to start building the habit. If you want to know more about radio remotes, visit some. Usually on weekends your local stations will have live remotes. Visit the business.

▼▼▼▼▼ GUARANTEED RESULTS ▼▼▼▼▼

See if they are getting good traffic. Ask people why they came to visit. The week after the remote call the business and ask them how it went. Ask them what they would do to improve it. Learn from their mistakes. As I have said many times, this is another time for having fun. Make the remote a party for everyone. Many times during remotes they will interview owners and managers. Be prepared - have what you want to say and the points you need to get across already written out so you do not become confused when you are on the air. Talk with the DJ's and make them feel comfortable. The more fun they have the more fun the listeners have.

Run Your Business The Way Your Customers Want It!

As I have said; The only reason you are in business is to help your customers meet their needs or solve their problems. Everything your business does affects your customers. For example, if you are only open from 10:00am to 11:00am and then 2:00pm to 4:00pm most people will not be able to get to your business during business hours. You see this often with government agencies. They are only open when you are at work. This makes it very hard to work with them. Take a moment and think of the changes you could make right now to accommodate your customers further. You should be able to think of at least one thing that you can do to make it easier on your customer. Maybe it's a night drop slot; maybe it's pick up and delivery; maybe it's something that you did five years ago and you stopped because you thought, "Ah, they don't care about that." But always try to go back and run your business the way the customer wants it to be run. If they want it to be open until midnight, you should try to find a way to

GUARANTEED RESULTS

service them. Maybe you can stay open until midnight two nights per week. Whatever you do make it easy for them.

Sales Reps "How could we hire sales reps, we cannot afford the staff we have now!" You can hire sales reps as 100% commission sales people. This means you only pay them if they make sales. This makes it a win-win situation. The more they sell the more they, and you, make. When you think of a sales rep keep in mind they may not work for you full time. Many times sales reps work with a number of complementary companies. This makes it easier for them to go out and sell a complete line of products or services. For example; you provide accounting services, you contract with a sales rep that sells complete business solutions. The sales person represents you, a lawyer, an ad agency and a temporary service. Every time the sales rep meets with a company, he analyzes what type of help they need and then makes a recommendation. Sometimes you will not be mentioned because they already have accounting help. When a sales rep works like this they are maximizing their time. This gives them a complete package to try to sell. If you do use a rep it is important to monitor the way they are representing your company. If they dress as a slob, people think that the work you do is sloppy. Also you need to take the time to educate this person about your company and the benefits your company has to offer. If you do not teach them they will never learn it. You want this person to make great money selling your products and services. Remember, the more they make the more you make. One last item, you can structure the compensation any way that you want to. Just one piece of advice; only pay the rep after

▼▼▼▼▼ GUARANTEED RESULTS ▼▼▼▼▼

you are paid in full by the client. Sales reps can provide many companies with the added sales push they need.

Selling The Back-End   All of us have information and items that other people want. When other people want them it means that you have a market in which to sell them. In your company it may be information or it may be a bi-product of your process. In your widget company you get leads from your marketing efforts of people that want to buy widgets. Would the person that sells widget financing or widget service like to have the name of the person that is looking to buy a new widget. Companies will sometimes pay over $100 for a "good" lead. What if you could sell this information and use it to offset some of your marketing expenses. Many times even list companies will buy the names and addresses you have generated.

Another example; what if in your widget making process you have waste wood. You could throw the wood in the trash or you could arrange for a recycling company to pay you for your waste. Or maybe some other company could use the wood for smaller items. Programs like these can be a wonderful way of increasing your marketing budget with no net cost to the company.

Making the most of your resources will often mean the difference between a profit or a loss. Always look for ways to take advantage of all of your opportunities.

Seminars   Seminars are a great way to educate your customers. Didn't we say at the beginning that education is a very important part of marketing? Seminars provide a great excuse for you to invite in your customers and prospective customers. You can invite them into your location or a neutral

▼▼▼▼▼ GUARANTEED RESULTS ▼▼▼▼▼

location, like a library. Most public libraries have rooms that you can use for a minimal fee. When I say "minimal"- $10-$15 a night. You can wheel in a cart of various beverages, iced tea, sodas and coffee. And you can help your customers learn about how to better use widgets and what everyone should know about widgets. Those seven or eight or ten people, or maybe fifty or a hundred, depending on the topic, are all good potential customers and they represent a great opportunity to have more people saying, "I really like those people at Widget World. They do a great job." Well, how does teaching them about widgets equate to you doing a great job? Very simple - perception. They perceive that from the experience they had in your seminar, you must be a caring person from a caring company. Earlier I talked about consistency, you cannot do one good and the other bad, because they will perceive that both are bad. So, you will have to make sure that you keep it on a level playing field; you have to make sure that you do everything right. But offer an opportunity for them to learn. Seminars are only limited by your imagination. If you cannot think of the best subject, call someone in your area, ask one of your friends, ask a significant other. Since you know your target market so well, ask them. If you want to do a seminar that is directed towards a specific group, get that group to say, "This is what we'd like to learn. This is what we'd like you to show us." And then do it. Again, nine times out of ten, you can do a seminar for next to nothing.

When you do a seminar you do not have to be the expert. Seminars can be very successful when you have someone else do the presentation. You can use suppliers or other professionals. For example, if you are a bank and you want more business customers and you want to use seminars as one of your tools you could bring in a

▼▼▼▼▼
GUARANTEED RESULTS
▼▼▼▼▼

CPA, lawyer, marketing consultant, tax advisor, etc. This gives your customer the idea that they will get good information from you and that you are there to help them. So be creative, think of what your customers want more information on and then present it.

You can solicit people to attend the seminar by telling all of your customers by mail and over the phone. You can run ads in targeted publications. I also recommend contacting the media so that they can mention how you are helping the community.

Start a Data Base For those of you who have not started a data base: shame on you. For those of you who have: use it! A data base is information on your customers and potential customers. Put one together. You can buy simple programs for your computer or you can set them up manually on cards. Just develop the information and use it. Even if it's just to send them a card four times a year--use it! The people that have purchased or have been into your business are golden. They have already shown that they will come to your place. They have already shown that they will purchase at your place. Hopefully, they have enjoyed the experience. That means that all you have to do is invite them back. Your data base should include; First Name, Last Name, Phone Number, Address, what they bought and any other information that is important to you. For example; Size of Company, Number of Children, Make of Automobile, Size of Home, etc.

▼▼▼▼▼
GUARANTEED RESULTS
▼▼▼▼▼

Start Marketing and Don't Ever Stop

It sounds a little silly, but many times what we run into are "Ahuh, I know March is going to be a slow month, so in February I'm really going to pull out all the stops. I will implement some of these new marketing tools and we will have a decent month." You then implement a few of the ideas and you limp through March, you think to yourself: "April and May always pick up, so I am going to go back to work and stop wasting my time on marketing." You go through a series of peaks and valleys. This is not the way you want to market your product or services. You want to put a marketing plan or calendar in place that you can "realistically" do every day. To be successful you need to do some marketing all the time. If you start today, you are going to get results sooner than if you start tomorrow. So, just start. It does not need to be full page ads. It can be as simple as just calling three past customers every day and saying hello. That will only take a few minutes each day and you will start getting your customers to think about you again! This generates "Top of Mind Awareness." This is a marketing term that means your customers are thinking about you and your products or services instead of other similar suppliers.

Start Promotions Early

Most businesses have certain seasonalities. Whether it's based on the holidays, or whether it's based on summer or whatever time of year, you have peaks and valleys. If you can get the person to spend their discretionary income with your business, before they spend it somewhere else, you have won. So try to get them to buy early. Give an incentive that says: "If you buy before Thanksgiving, we

▼▼▼▼▼
GUARANTEED RESULTS
▼▼▼▼▼

will give you 'x' or we have a special for you of 'y'". The reason being: after Thanksgiving, everyone else is trying to get their money. But, if you already have your share of it, you have won. You will see this with automobile dealerships, they are starting their model close out earlier and earlier. They know that if their customer purchases from them now, they have one less unit in inventory that they will not have to discount later. You need to look at it the same way. If most of your customers purchase in the fall give them an incentive to buy from you in the summer. That is the idea behind "buy now and pay later." They know that they have made their sale and all they need to do is collect the money and many times the interest as well.

Stickers Stickers, stickers, stickers -- stickers are great. People love them. Bumper stickers, stickers on envelopes, stickers on their products, stickers on whatever. Put the name of your company on a very nice sticker on the bottom of all the widgets you produce. This helps your customers remember where they purchased it; so they can come back when they have a problem and you can get service. This is a very simple inexpensive marketing tool you can use and many people never think of it. You can use stickers to announce sales or next month's special or just to say thank you. Stickers are often very inexpensive and very effective. This is a marketing tool that all business should use!

Suggestive Selling Suggestive selling or educational selling is the easiest sales process. It puts you in the situation where you get to say to your customer, "Did you know?" "Did you know that this does this and this

▼
87

and this, and this is why it helps you?" "Did you know that our product or our processing has this and this, and that is why it helps you?" Doing this makes the customer feel like: "I'm learning something; these people are smart; I want to buy from them." Again, you are putting yourself in an authoritative position as opposed to negotiating price. Try to stay away from negotiating price as best as you can. The other part of suggestive selling or any selling that's important is to get as much information from the customer as you can, that way you can better explain how your product or service will help them. An important point to remember about selling is asking questions and listening. It is very hard to listen too much.

Surveys and Questionnaires

Always ask your customers what they like and what they do not like. Sometimes what they are going to tell you is a lie. But ask them any way. The reason I say it's a lie is because they will over think: "Well, how was my last experience?" And they will have a hard time filling it out. But try to get that information. Always ask them about new products or services that they want and what they will pay for it. It does not have to be formal. I do a lot of "mother-in-law" surveys. Those are the surveys where you ask your mother-in-law what she thinks. Ask three or four people, "Is it statistically significant?" No. But it's better than just having one person guess. Surveys and questionnaires give you better information to make decisions. The better informed you are, the better your chances are of making a good decision. If you do not feel comfortable doing the survey, you can often hire a marketing student to do it for you. They may even use it as a class project.

▼▼▼▼▼
GUARANTEED RESULTS
▼▼▼▼▼

Telemarketing Some people think this is the biggest sin ever. Other people love it because it helps them to make a profit. If you do it, do a good job at it. As I mentioned before, tell the truth and listen to what your customers are saying. One of the best ways to telemarket is to hire an outside service. They have the people and they know how to do it and get results. If you do hire a telemarketing firm, do your homework. If the company you hire is not professional, you can end up with no sales and angry customers. Talk with some of their current customers, ask how their customers reacted. If you choose to do the telemarketing yourself the first point to remember is that most people will say NO and many will be rude! When you develop your script for your calls make it simple, make it brief, explain how they will benefit, tell them what you want them to do and then get on with it. Time is precious, so respect that.

Telemarketing is a great marketing tool to use with direct mail. Your response will increase significantly by following up your mailing with phone calls.

Telephone Answering Scripts How do you greet people? How do you answer the phone? I believe whole heartedly in scripting. Not to the point that it sounds stilted or unnatural, we have all heard those. Rather scripts that help your people to get the benefit of your product or service out quickly and easily. You have about thirty seconds to make an impression; hopefully you make a good one. So give your people an idea of what to say. We have all been in a situation where we have to hire or work with people who may not be as qualified or as well trained as we would like, so give them

▼▼▼▼▼ GUARANTEED RESULTS ▼▼▼▼▼

easy materials to work with. Give them the benefits - one, two, three. Give them the points you want to get across on the phone so they can do it. Also, it's important to remember, what is good for the goose is good for the gander. Too many times we say, "Well, I run the company, I know how to answer the phone - I'll do it my way." As soon as they see or hear you, they are going to mimic it. So have a script - use it - it works for everyone!

Ten Arounds This is a very simple and effective way of promoting your business to your target market. Ten arounds mean that anytime your company works with a client you canvass the ten businesses or homes around that customer. It is based on the simple premise that we have similarities to our neighbors. If one home in a area needs a new roof, others will also. Because the homes were usually built around the same time. The same holds true for businesses in an office park. They all pay similar rents they will have some of the same needs. This can be amazingly effective for all businesses.

This is an excellent time to start using door hangers. You can just walk around the area and introduce new people to your products or services. You can also use this information to buy your targeted mailing list. You can either buy names of people and businesses in that area or you can use that area as a model to match against.

Testing In everything you do in your business you should test. Too many times people make important and expensive decisions based on guesses. You want to test everything you do. I will talk about testing from your marketing stand point but you need to also look at testing in other areas of your business as well. Have you ever written a letter and

▼▼▼▼▼ GUARANTEED RESULTS ▼▼▼▼▼

said, "This is going to generate a big response!" Did it? Could the response have been better? The only way to know the answer to these questions is to test. You should test your ads, your letters, your telephone scripts. For example; Develop an ad and see what your response is. Now that you know how many people called or came in, change the headline - only the headline. Did more people come in or buy? Once you develop the ad that gets the best response use that as your control. Control means the baseline that all other headlines are tested against. If your control headline produces a 5% response and your new headline produces a 2% response you stay with the control. Now once you develop a headline that gets better response than the control, it then becomes the new control. Testing is the only systematic way to improve your results.

Thank You Notes and Letters

When someone spends their hard earned money in your business, thank them. Keep in mind that whether it is a company or an individual, they worked hard for their money that they are spending in your business. Thank you notes are a great way of reminding them that "You appreciate their business". A little bit of appreciation may be all you need to get them in the door a second or third time--or, perhaps the forty-fifth time. Again though, be consistent. One of the worst things you can do is send out thank you notes one time and not the next. If you are going to do it, either everyone that purchases gets a thank you. Or set a dollar volume - that anything over an "x" purchase, gets a thank you note. Make sure that everyone with over that purchase receives one! Remember, people understand consistency and if I get one when I bought the $250

▼▼▼▼▼ GUARANTEED RESULTS ▼▼▼▼▼

VCR, and I did not get one the time I bought the $250 widget. I say, "What? Don't they like me anymore?" So, send them out always. All of your customers are people. Sometimes we forget that, we become so myopic; we become so focused and forget the fact that our customers are people. And they want to be treated the way any other person would want to be treated.

Tracking and Monitoring

Always keep track of your marketing efforts. It really scares me when people do not. When they say, "I sent out a mailer and it did okay." What defines okay? How many people came in from it? How many dollars did you generate? What have your sales done for the next thirty, sixty, ninety days? Because you are going to have some residual effects, you need to track. These types of things help you to make better decisions next time. We all make mistakes. People who try new ways, make mistakes. But the smart ones learn from those mistakes and turn them into positives and say, "Hey, this mailer didn't get the people I wanted, but it did generate interest from these people - How can I do it better?" So, really track and monitor. Develop a very simple system, just mark on a notepad what marketing tool you used and what the results have been.

Traffic Patterns

There are two main types of traffic patterns; inside your location and outside your location. Where do people go when they are in your establishment? Do they go where you want them to? Could you arrange things better so that you can get those incremental sales more easily? Grocery stores set up fun items right by the check-out. That is done for a reason. It's called

▼▼▼▼▼ GUARANTEED RESULTS ▼▼▼▼▼

impulse buying. So people can buy a magazine and gum every time they go to the store! That's just money on the top for them. You should do the same. Do not make it cluttered, make it so the people walk by those things that they can easily purchase. This is a great way to generate incremental sales. Have the items that people need but always forget, in places where they cannot miss them. Our local grocery stores are now putting up signs that say, "Don't forget the ice!" That is a perfect way to increase the sale of ice because most people do not think of it even though they need it. If you know the internal traffic patterns of your store you can better meet your client's needs. If you want to know the traffic patterns act as a customer and follow your next ten customers around. Watch what they do, where they go and where they stop. This will give you a good start.

The other traffic pattern is outside your location. How many people go by your business every day? How many of your target customers go by each day? How could you get more of them to just stop in? How can you get more of the people that go to the business next to yours to come into your business? What can you do to make it easier for your customers; more parking, lighted parking, covered parking, easier access to the street, better signage, etc. Again the best inexpensive way to monitor your traffic pattern is to sit out and watch the cars. And ask people when they come in about getting to your business. These are all pieces of the successful business puzzle. The more you know, the better you will be able to serve your customer.

Trial Size and Sampling

I am asked over and over should we give "FREE" samples. My answer is YES. As a marketing driven company you know that you need to get

▼▼▼▼▼ GUARANTEED RESULTS ▼▼▼▼▼

people to try your product or service and one of the best ways to do that is with a free trial. The sample can be very small or if you provide a service it may be a very limited use of your service. When you provide a sample or trial offer you enable the customer to see the benefit of your product so strongly that they cannot help purchasing. Once you show someone that your product or service works, they are in an excellent position to purchase. Sampling and trials are strong marketing tools. You need to get people in the habit of purchasing your product or service. The way to do that is with free trial samples. Give your customer and potential customers the opportunity to experience your product or service. If along with the experience you educate them, you are well on your way to a sale and hopefully a good long term relationship. Are you investing time and money to do that? Yes. But, hopefully, you're going to get them to say, "Hey, this was great. I want to come back and do it again." The reason you get those little detergents in the mail is not because they think your clothes are dirty. It's because they want you to try it and say, "This is great". And then go out and buy the product. You can do the same thing- everyone can trial or sample.

Two-for ... Two-for, three-for! Two-fors are great. People love them. With offers like these people perceive that they are getting something for nothing. These are a great way for you to increase your average dollars per transaction. For example, if people usually by one widget at a time offer, "Buy two widgets get the third one free!" You are increasing the purchase to two at a time. Will all of your customers take advantage of this offer? No. But some of them will and guess what? You have just increased your sales. Again a program like this is

▼▼▼▼▼ GUARANTEED RESULTS ▼▼▼▼▼

limited only by your imagination. Two for the price of one; five for the price of two. Just try it.

Use Shoppers   Hire someone or have someone you know, who is not employed by you necessarily, go out and look at the competitions' products and services, and then write down objectively what they have seen or experienced. It's amazing how many businesses I walk into and it's as if red lights go off when I see things that are done incorrectly from a marketing perspective. Have someone else observe for you. Many times you can get someone- -- a friend or family member to do it. Have them go to a competitor, buy their widget. What did they say? What did they do? What did you like? What didn't you like? They can give you a lot of good information and ways to improve your business. You should also make it a point to talk with and visit your direct competitors regularly. How can you compete and win if you do not know what your competitor is doing.

Value Packaging   Many times you can develop a group of products that complement each other and sell them as a "Special Value Package." This allows you to increase the amount of your average sale as well as putting you in the position of selling complete solutions. You can put together a group of products or services and offer the complete package at a discounted price. Automobile manufacturers are doing this all the time. They refer to them as option packages. They know that most people want electric windows and power locks so they develop an option package that includes them. The price for power windows and locks may be $500. In the option package you get power

▼▼▼▼▼ GUARANTEED RESULTS ▼▼▼▼▼

windows, power locks, power mirrors, trunk release and cruise control all for only $650. This package allows the car maker to increase your order by $150 and the cost to them is very little. Adding $150 per car has a significant impact on the bottom line of any company. Another industry that is currently using this technique is the software industry. They refer to it as "bundling". They may "bundle" their software with a computer or they may bundle 3 packages together at a discounted price. Microsoft is doing this with some of their products now. They are selling complete office solutions; word processor, spread sheet, data base and graphics package all for a portion of what you would normally pay if sold separately. They know that if you shop around you may buy the other products from other companies. By doing this they know that you are almost locked into the use of Microsoft products. You should be doing the same thing with your products and services. Look for natural groupings of your products and services. When you look at your widget think of the other pieces that should be included with it. You may now sell the "Super Widget Package"; it includes one super widget, batteries, cables, service for two years and a carrying case all for the price of the widget and the case. You have increased your average sale and they are locked in to you for service. Whether you call it bundling or packaging it very simply means providing a complete solution for your customer's needs. It is great for both you and your customer. They get a discount on a complete solution and you have increased sales. This is definitely a win-win situation.

Watch Trends Not just in your industry, but in your community, as well as in the country. What are people doing now? When bungy jumping was big- -- you could have thought "can

▼
96

▼▼▼▼▼ GUARANTEED RESULTS ▼▼▼▼▼

we provide widgets to bungy jumpers better than someone else? Maybe we could do a premium product with bungy jumpers." Those types of things are an excellent way to become known in a market; to develop a personality of your own; and to succeed. Watch the trends and what is going on.

When You Talk To Your Customers, Always Describe The Benefits, Not The Features

In case you have not noticed I think this is very important. If you choose only to apply one of the ideas expressed in this book please make it this one. Your customers do not care about you! They care about how you will satisfy their needs or solve their problems. That is all. So when you tell people that you just spent $10,000,000 on a new facility, guess what, they do not care. If that facility can now give them better widgets, quicker turn around, more choices, better prices, these are the points they care about. In all of your marketing, which is all your business does now, think, talk and describe your products and services in a way that describes how the customer benefits.

Work With Your Community

All of us need to give back to our communities. In today's difficult times we need to look at how we can help others. One of the best ways to do this is to talk with the people who are in your community; find groups who need your help. When you find a group, make sure that you also want to help them. This is going to take some of your time and maybe even some of your money so make it something you enjoy and want to do. There are always

▼▼▼▼▼ GUARANTEED RESULTS ▼▼▼▼▼

people out there that need your help. One of the areas that I recommend serving in is "career day". It sounds kind of goofy. Go out to "career days" at your local schools. It's amazing how many of those students and their families remember what you do. And it's amazing how many of the teacher's families say, "Well, I should go into Widget World because he cares and he gives back to the community." You can also work with your community. You can also join one of the service clubs like Rotary. This is an excellent way to meet people, help others that need your help and to have more people learn about Widget World.

Yellow Pages The Yellow Pages are one of the best places for many businesses to advertise. When a potential customer picks up the Yellow Pages they are looking for a solution to a problem. They may be needing new tires, a restaurant or a dentist. What is important to remember is that this potential customer wants a solution NOW! By advertising in the Yellow Pages you are putting yourself in position to make that sale. If you run an ad in the Yellow Pages you want to look at it from the same perspective you would any other marketing effort. What does my customer want and what problems are they trying to solve. Now that you know this you can develop an ad that will be effective for you. Always start out with a strong headline and have a call to action. If you have to choose between a larger ad or one that uses color I always recommend that you use the color. Using red will often make your ad stand out from every other ad on the page. Make sure you have Yellow Pages as one of the marketing areas that you track the results of.

GUARANTEED RESULTS

80/20 Rule   Plan your marketing using the 80/20 rule. Most companies get 80% of their business from 20% of their clients. Most get 80% of their problems from 20% of their clients. You should spend 80% of your time and money on the 20% of your clients that make up 80% of your revenue. If you spend most of your time and money on the people that are currently buying your product or service you will be well ahead of the game. Too many times people spend their time and money on the people who are not buying.

You will need to dedicate some of your budget for new product introductions and for expansion into new markets; but you never want to walk away from your current customers. It is too costly these days to spend money that does not generate results. The 80/20 rule is not cast in concrete. For many of our clients we break it down 70/20/10. 70% of our time and money on current customers, 20% on the most likely candidates and 10% on new markets or the universe. If you plan your marketing this way you will often see much better results than you have in the past.

▼▼▼▼▼ GUARANTEED RESULTS ▼▼▼▼▼

Questions Here you have it, the following are answers to some of your favorite marketing questions.

When Should I Advertise? The simple answer to this is before and while you need the business. The better answer is it depends on your business. You need to plan your advertising, and all marketing efforts, well in advance. Most magazines need to have your camera-ready art as much as 60 days in advance. They may need you to reserve your space as much as 120 days in advance. So if you think you need to advertise now, it may be 4 months before you can get your ad in the magazine.

The most direct answer to this question is you want to advertise when your customer needs your product or service to solve their problem. If you are selling heaters it is very difficult to get people in Florida interested in them in July. In a situation like this you would want to start your advertising before the season so your customers and potential customers can start thinking about how your product will help them keep warm this winter. Then once it starts getting cold you want to be in front of your target all the time. After the season is over you can run discount promotions.

This can be a very difficult question. You need to think about when your customers and potential customers most likely need your service. That is always the best time to advertise.

Keep in mind the importance of repetition, breaking through the clutter, and letting them know how they will benefit from your product or service. These points may be more important than the best time to run an ad.

▼▼▼▼▼ GUARANTEED RESULTS ▼▼▼▼▼

What Can I Do To Make My Ads Work Better?

The best way to make your ads work better is to know your customer better. The more you know about them and what is important to them the easier it is to develop effective ads. The first part of an ad read is the headline. So the best way to make your ad more effective is to have a headline that stops your customer, makes them want to read the rest of the ad and gets a vivid picture of how your product or service is going to help them.

The second part that many ads do not have is a `call to action'. You need to tell the reader what to do and when to do it. Too many times people produce ads that are very pretty and fun but do not tell the reader what to do next. You want your ad to have a strong call to action, i.e. "Call now to find out how Widget World can start saving you money." "Stop in today to see how our widgets will make your life easier."

The next important part of your ad is the appearance. You want your ad to reflect positively on your company and you also want it to be easy to read. You want to select a type face and size that makes it simple for the reader to read.

Another way to make your ads more effective is to go through the marketing questionnaire in the back of the book. These questions will help you get the most important information so that you can include it in your ad.

You also need to test. Every ad can perform better. The only way to find this out is by testing. When you test always start with the headline. Change the headline and see if you get more traffic and people who are more likely to purchase. Sometimes just by making changes in your headline you can see drastic

▼▼▼▼▼ GUARANTEED RESULTS ▼▼▼▼▼

improvements in your advertising results. You always want to find your customer's hot button. Testing your headlines is one of the best ways to do this. You can even test a series of ads at the same time. Just put different phone numbers in each ad or have the people ask for a fictitious person. You can then, very confidently, tell how many calls were generated by each ad or each headline. Try to keep them simple and direct and many times you will find that you have a winner.

How Do I Get A write-up In My Local Newspaper?

To be written up in your local paper you need to provide them with a news story. When I say news story I mean information that people in your community would find interesting and would like to know more about. Simply saying you are having a sale is not news in most communities. Announcing that you have a new President or that you have announced that you will now have only one sale per year is news.

Being published or mentioned by the media is up to the media's discretion. If they like the idea or concept you are in, if they do not, you are out. When you are thinking about being in the media you need to develop a complete concept of how the story relates to the media and why they should see it as newsworthy.

Another important part of working with the media is getting to know them and having them get to know you. You need to do your homework. You need to develop a list of the writers and editors who are most likely to be interested in a story that relates to your business. These people are very busy and they are bombarded with many story ideas everyday. If you have done your job correctly, you know them and they

GUARANTEED RESULTS

know you, it improves the chances of them using your information. One other point to remember is that if you have a history of providing them with good newsworthy information, they will be more likely to listen to you next time.

Include photographs, if your paper runs some of their pictures in color you may want to provide both color and black and white prints. On the back of the photograph always include; company name, address, phone number, contact person and a brief description of the photograph. When you supply a photo the chances of you being selected goes up exponentially.

You should provide them with; who, what, when, where, why and how. This is the information that they want and need to make decisions on the story items to pursue and to write a good story.

What Is The Difference Between Marketing And Advertising?

Many people are confused by these two terms. Because some people use them synonymously. Well, they are not.

Marketing is the entire umbrella that covers everything a company does to get their products or services sold. It includes advertising as well as distribution, sales, public relations, pricing, packaging, etc.

Advertising is the development and placement of ads to increase the awareness and sales of a product or service. One important point to note about advertising is that you pay for the placement of your information. You also decide what it's going to say and how it will be said. Advertising is just one small piece of the marketing pie.

Everyone needs to use marketing but not everyone needs to advertise. We all need to generate interest in

GUARANTEED RESULTS

our products and services but we may not need to do that with ads. You may do it with other tools like public relations, seminars, etc.

How Do You Know If You Need An Advertising Agency?

Too many times people hire an ad agency because one of their friends at the club did, or they have a friend that owns one. You want to start using an ad agency when you need one. It is not unlike hiring any outside help for your business. You would hire accounting help or a CPA when you and your people can no longer handle the company's accounting needs. The same is true for hiring an ad agency. When you cannot develop the ads that make your clients and prospects react the way they should you should start looking for an agency.

Also keep in mind media buying. You may be able to generate the ads OK but you realize that you are not buying effective media. That is the time to start looking.

As a follow-up to this question I am often asked should we do it ourselves or hire an agency. My answer to this question is to hire a staff of educated people to develop the ads, produce the ads, and place them, you are going to need a fairly large budget. People with this level of education and talent are not cheap. Also with the advancement in technology the initial investment for some of the equipment may be more than your entire annual advertising budget.

The best way to get a good agency is to develop a positive working relationship over time. Your advertising is too important not do a good job. Often this is the first impression a person has of your company.

▼▼▼▼▼
GUARANTEED RESULTS
▼▼▼▼▼

What Does An Advertising Agency Do For Me?

This depends on what you want them to do for you and the agency you decide to work with. The minimum any good agency should do is help you develop a positive consistent image for your products and services.

Normally your ad agency will help you develop ads that will get your customers and potential customers to take action. They will also help you with the placement of the ads. Your agency will help with the selection of media to work in conjunction with your ads to get the most interest from your customers and potential customers.

From a media stand point an ad agency is able to offer the advantage of using their size and other clients to negotiate better rates for you. For example, you may want to run a half page ad in Newsweek. Your media rep will quote you a rate off the rate card. If the media department at the agency talks to Newsweek they may be able to tell them they have five clients looking to put ads in the magazine, thus how much of a discount will we get. That is a very good bargaining tool for the agency to use. Also they can get special perks for their clients, i.e., premium positioning or service charges waived.

Ad agencies are a helping hand. They are not a savior. They function much like a computer, garbage in, garbage out. If you work with them, give them good information and good direction, you can have some amazingly positive results.

GUARANTEED RESULTS

Can I Negotiate Advertising Space Rates?

If you would like to you sure can try to negotiate your space rates. All rates are negotiable. One of the points that you want to remember is that you may need the publication's help someday! Negotiating media rates can be fun if you like to negotiate. If you do not like to negotiate you may want to consider either using an ad agency, marketing firm or a media buying service. They will all help you get the best rates possible for your media dollar.

Please keep in mind that no matter how little you pay for the media if it does not reach YOUR target, the people you want to see it, you are wasting your money. Also, as you negotiate you should negotiate based on cost to reach your potential customers, not the entire world.

Negotiating is an art some people are good at it and others are not. All you have to lose is the time you spend trying to get better rates.

If You Only Had $50 To Spend On Advertising What Would You Do?

I would spend it on my current customers. I would start with the five or ten best customers that I have and I would try to get them to purchase either again or a larger dollar amount. I would send them a letter and then do a follow up call. The letter would emphasize the benefit of my product or service as well as educate them on why NOW is the best time to buy. The follow-up call would serve as a reminder and ask them to come visit.

I would also do a $20 and $10 internal sales incentive for the people that generate the highest dollar volume of widgets for the next 3 weeks.

▼▼▼▼▼ GUARANTEED RESULTS ▼▼▼▼▼

You need to look at your business and your customers for the best answer to that question but start out looking at your current customers first. You will get your best results with your least investment. Also look in the front of the book at the entire list of marketing tools and you decide the best ones for you to implement that are under $50.

Try not to put yourself in the situation of only having $50 to spend. Develop your budget, stick to it, and always work to improve the results of your marketing. This will help get you out of the $50 advertising rut.

How Do I Get People To Come Into My Business?

Provide good service, make their buying experience wonderful. The best way to get people to come into your business is from repeat customers. They can provide good word of mouth advertising as well as repeat purchasing.

Possibly the most important part of generating increased traffic is very simply making your business more visible. You need to do everything in your power to make your signage big and easy to read. Think about whether your customers will be walking or driving by. Look at what they can see. You may need to cut down a tree or move your sign to make it easier to see. If people are walking by, make it inviting to come in. Many times just having the front door open will help. Customers will see that you are open and will just come in. Make it bright and fun looking. Also having balloons or something that is eye catching will help. If people usually just walk by, consider having someone out front handing out samples or inviting people in.

Make it special. Give them a good reason to come in. "Welcome" is an invitation but is not a good reason.

▼▼▼▼▼
GUARANTEED RESULTS
▼▼▼▼▼

Give them a benefit reason to come in. For example; We will save you $$$$. We will help you be happier than you have ever been before. Explain and educate people why they need to come into your business.

What Should I Budget For Advertising/Marketing?

If you are thinking about a budget for your advertising and marketing you are much better than most people. Too many people just want to guess at what they need to spend.

Two good ways of setting your budget are by basing your budget on a percentage of sales or basing it on results.

The percentage of sales system works by banking a percentage of your sales for marketing. For example some industries put as little as .5%. Other industries may bank as much as 20% for marketing. The reason they vary is due to the amount of profit they have in the product or service as well as what marketing they need to do to generate sales. In business to business sales the percentage that is used for marketing is usually lower than cosmetics for example, where the percentage is very high. The negative side to budgeting this way is that if your sales start to decline or flatten out your marketing budget will do the same. Now you are putting yourself in a situation where your sales are declining and so is your marketing budget, so you spend less and you get fewer sales, so you spend less and sales go down more. This can be a very bad position to be in. In a situation like this you need to re-think the idea of percentage of sales.

The results method is the way I prefer but it is also the most difficult. What the results method does is say we will pay for sales results not advertising or public relations. This means that if you do not sell much you

▼▼▼▼▼ GUARANTEED RESULTS ▼▼▼▼▼

are not going to pay very much. If your sales increase 100% your marketing expenses are also increasing. The best way to think of this is if your widgets sell for $3.00 and your cost is $.50, you could spend $.50 for results on every widget you sell. What you then need to do is look at the advertising and marketing you want to do and start negotiating with the people to make this work.

Should I Use Expiration Dates On My Promotional Offers?

Yes! No question about it. Always have an expiration date on all of your marketing materials. This creates urgency. We need to tell people what we want them to do and why they should do it. We also need to tell them when to do it. A great way to do this is with expiration dates.

I am also often asked, "Should I accept expired coupons?" Yes! Explain to the customer that this has expired but you would like for them to take advantage of the offer and just this once you will make an exception. You want them to be happy. If it means making good on an expired offer I would always do it. Explain very clearly that this is the only time you will do it but you value their business.

How Do I Create Urgency?

Expiration dates are a good way to create urgency. Urgency is created when you have a limit. It may be limited time, limited quantity, limited to the first 100 people, limited ... You may have 200 widgets to sell over the next two days. We will only sell 100 widgets each of the next two days.

▼▼▼▼▼ GUARANTEED RESULTS ▼▼▼▼▼

This creates the perception that if they want one of your widgets they better act now.

An important part of creating urgency is telling people about the urgency. If you are only selling 100 per day, educate your people that they need to tell every customer that Widget World will only sell 100 per day. This makes people that do not want to decide make a decision. They know that if they do not buy now they may be out of luck. After someone tells me that, even if I was not looking for a widget, I may think about getting one because they are limited.

In all of your marketing efforts you want to create urgency. The more urgent you make it the better and faster your marketing effort will go.

What Is The Best Way To Cold Call?

Don't do it. Have public relations and other tools working for you so people know you. If the person has heard of your business, it makes it much easier to talk with them. They may not have met you but they know your company name. If you can immediately develop some rapport with the person you are talking with you are not really cold calling.

When you are forced to make cold calls lead with the benefit. Tell the person what you will do for them. This is what they want to know. Do not try to be cute and evasive, tell them up front how they will benefit from this call. After you have them interested you can now start asking questions and explain how your product or service will solve their specific problems.

If you are going to be doing cold calling, develop a script and routine for your sales process. You want to know what works best so you do not waste your time on words and routines that do not produce. Once you have developed the best way for you to make cold calls

GUARANTEED RESULTS

write it down so that you and others can do it the same way every time. Do not waste time making other people learn how to do it on their own. Let them learn from your mistakes. You are cold calling to generate business. Develop the words that work best for you and use them every time.

What Are The Most Important Parts Of Marketing?

I do not know if this really answers the question but here goes. For any person the best place to start with marketing is with a good product or service that meets a customer's needs. If you start with meeting your customers needs you will be way ahead of many people.

Now you need to make the most of every opportunity and tell your target audience, most likely customers, over and over how they will benefit from your product or service. Your customer does not care about you. They care about themselves. They want to know what you are going to do for them. If you stress the benefits and advantages to them in a way that they understand you are going to be doing well.

Lastly, you need to stand out from the clutter. We are all becoming more and more busy. We see hundreds of marketing messages every day. You need to have your message stand out in a positive manner. Many times when you look through a newspaper's classified section, you will see an ad with a headline that just says, "SEX." They got your attention, they cut through the clutter, but did they give you a benefit? Did that put their company in a positive light? You need to make those decisions. But you do need to stand out. You should look at shapes, colors and size as a good place to start for standing out.

▼▼▼▼▼
GUARANTEED RESULTS
▼▼▼▼▼

What Do You Do When People Call Or Stop In And Ask Price?

These people are tire kickers or price shoppers. You need to have a sales routine or script for this situation. Everyone gets these calls. You need to very quickly and simply explain that the benefits of your products or services make price less important. You want to explain that they not only get a widget they get service, the best name in widgets, a 10 year guarantee and widgets that are made in the US. Now you can say other people may sell cheaper widgets but you get what you pay for. You need to know what other people are selling so you can explain why yours is the best VALUE.

The reason people ask about price is it is very easy to understand. They understand that $6 is more than $5. You need to explain why $6 is a better value and a better buy by showing the customer the benefits that your product or service provides them. If you know people are going to price shop explain to them what they will be seeing, what are the tricks that other people are trying to use. Be up front. Ask people if they have looked other places. You need to help educate people why price is not the most important issue in buying your product or service.

How Do We Get People In During Our Slow Times?

Start planning your marketing early to help avoid slow times, if you are in an industry that has a slow season. Maybe you sell ice in Alaska, and in the winter not too many people are buying it. You need to think of reasons that people will need your product in slow times. You may want to educate your customers why ice is so important and better than the

GUARANTEED RESULTS

alternative. A good example of this is companies that sell bottled water. For many years people used the water that came out of the faucet in the kitchen for drinking. After years of education many people now think the only water that is good to drink is bottled water. Education is an excellent way to help promote your business during slow times.

Another good way to increase business during slow times is with discount offers. I live in Arizona and the resorts, restaurants and golf courses have learned that you need to give a reason for people to come and use your product or service when it is hot outside. You will find resorts that reduce their rates from $250 per night to as little as $65 in the summer. They know that by doing this people will come stay at the resort. The resort can make money on dinners, drinks and other services they provide. Travel planners are now recommending people visit Arizona in the summer because of the great pricing. You can do similar tests with your business.

What Do You Do With Angry Customers?

If you make customer service a priority hopefully you will reduce the number of unhappy customers you will have. When you do have a problem with a customer, here are some important points to remember.

- When you have an unhappy customer do not get angry with them.
- Listen to what they have to say and how they would like to solve the problem.
- Do not get in an argument with them.
- Ask them how they see resolving the problem.

GUARANTEED RESULTS

- Apologize for the problem. Take ownership. Do not pass the buck.
- Work to come to a resolution that both parties will be happy with.
- Do not say, "That is not our problem." It is your problem if your customer thinks it is your problem.
- Send a note apologizing for the problem.

You need to be prepared for the situation of unhappy customers. It will happen in every business. Many times it is through no fault of yours. You need to develop a program for how unhappy customers will be handled and educate everyone in your company what they need to do. Many times people just want the chance to talk with a manager or owner. They are looking for the opportunity to vent their frustrations. You need to have your employees prepared for the situation and educate them that the frustration is not with them, it is with the situation. They need to know not to take it personally. Everyone is working towards the same goal and that is a satisfied happy customer.

GUARANTEED RESULTS

Important Marketing Information

1. The purpose of this marketing effort is:
2. The person, target customer that I want to educate is:
3. The buying decision will be made by:
4. Others who will affect the buying decision are:
5. My product or service does:
6. The single most important benefit (to my customer) of my product or service is:
7. Other benefits that must be emphasized are:
8. Other important benefits are:
9. Do not include the following:
10. What single benefit is going to make the target customer take action:
11. What are the biggest problems this product or service solves for the customer:
12. How knowledgeable is my customer:
    Very   Moderate   Low
13. Who are my strongest competitors:
14. How do their products or services compare with mine:
15. What is the state of the art of our product or service:
    Leader   Middle   Low
16. Do I have any exclusives:
17. What other background materials are available: Brochures, sales sheets, etc.
18. Any suggestions regarding copy approach:
19. The publications that I know my target reads are:

Also keep in mind the following!

Lead with the solution or benefit the customer wants!
Call to action. What and when do you want them to do!
Headline (Use answers 10, 12, 6 & 7)
P.S. and bullet points have high readership!
Breadth of services that you provide.

▼▼▼▼▼
GUARANTEED RESULTS
▼▼▼▼▼

Implementation Form

Please use this area to write down the top 5 tools that you want to implement for *Guaranteed Results*!

Tool #1 (Name) ....
Budget? (Set your budget) ....
Set your GOAL? (Be specific) ....
Who will be involved? (List everyone, both internal and external people) ....
What are you trying to accomplish? (Be specific) ......
When is it going to happen? (Set due dates for each part of this marketing effort) ....
Where is it going to happen? ....
Why are you doing this? (The more specific you are the better the results will be) ....
How are you going to do this ....
Explain & Educate (All of your internal and external people) ....

▼▼▼▼▼ GUARANTEED RESULTS ▼▼▼▼▼

Tool #2 (Name)..
Budget? (Set your budget)..................................
Set your GOAL? (Be specific)..............................
Who will be involved? (List everyone, both internal and external people)...
What are you trying to accomplish? (Be specific)...........
When is it going to happen? (Set due dates for each part of this marketing effort)......................................
Where is it going to happen? ....
Why are you doing this? (The more specific you are the better the results will be) ....
How are you going to do this.............................
Explain & Educate (All of your internal and external people) ....

▼▼▼▼▼ GUARANTEED RESULTS ▼▼▼▼▼

Tool #3 (Name)
Budget? (Set your budget)..
Set your GOAL? (Be specific)..
Who will be involved? (List everyone, both internal and external people)..
What are you trying to accomplish? (Be specific)...........
When is it going to happen? (Set due dates for each part of this marketing effort)..
Where is it going to happen? ....
Why are you doing this? (The more specific you are the better the results will be) ....
How are you going to do this..
Explain & Educate (All of your internal and external people) ....

▼▼▼▼▼
GUARANTEED RESULTS
▼▼▼▼▼

Tool #4(Name)..
Budget? (Set your budget)...
Set your GOAL? (Be specific)...
Who will be involved? (List everyone, both internal and external people)..
What are you trying to accomplish? (Be specific)............
When is it going to happen? (Set due dates for each part of this marketing effort)..
Where is it going to happen? ....
Why are you doing this? (The more specific you are the better the results will be) ....
How are you going to do this..
Explain & Educate (All of your internal and external people) ....

▼▼▼▼▼ GUARANTEED RESULTS ▼▼▼▼▼

Notes Section   Please use this area to write down notes and ideas that you have as you read *Guaranteed Results*!

▼▼▼▼▼
GUARANTEED RESULTS
▼▼▼▼▼

Please use this area to write down notes and ideas that you have as you read *Guaranteed Results*!

▼▼▼▼▼
GUARANTEED RESULTS
▼▼▼▼▼

Please use this area to write down notes and ideas that you have as you read *Guaranteed Results!*

▼▼▼▼▼
GUARANTEED RESULTS
▼▼▼▼▼

Please use this area to write down notes and ideas that you have as you read *Guaranteed Results*!

▼▼▼▼▼ GUARANTEED RESULTS ▼▼▼▼▼

Please use this area to write down notes and ideas that you have as you read *Guaranteed Results!*

▼▼▼▼▼
GUARANTEED RESULTS
▼▼▼▼▼

Please use this area to write down notes and ideas that you have as you read *Guaranteed Results*!

▼▼▼▼▼
GUARANTEED RESULTS
▼▼▼▼▼

Martin R. Baird

Author Information

Martin has a wonderful way of looking at everything from a marketing perspective. He is always asking questions because he knows that the more questions he asks the closer he gets to the answer. Marketing is about finding out what your customer wants and then finding how to tell them you have it.

He was born and raised in Indiana. He attended Purdue University where he majored in Communications Advertising with a minor in Marketing.

An experienced, trail-blazing marketing professional whose accomplishments include designing unique, trend-setting marketing programs, Martin has worked with companies like Bristol Corporation, Motorola, Executone and Microtest just to name a few. His love for marketing is exemplified by wanting to help smaller companies learn how to be more marketing driven and more competitive.

He founded Robinson & Associates, a full-service marketing management firm, in Scottsdale, Arizona. Robinson & Associates has won opportunities to represent some of the area's finest, most progressive businesses. Robinson & Associates clients range from fortune 100 companies to entrepreneurial startups. Clients currently are from coast to coast.

Martin is a talented project coordinator with the ability to produce top-quality marketing materials while providing "Extra Mile Service."

He is an experienced presenter and lecturer. His seminars include all areas of marketing and range from international and national audiences to regional and local. Martin enjoys participating in corporate

▼▼▼▼▼ GUARANTEED RESULTS ▼▼▼▼▼

sponsored seminars that are designed to "help businesses succeed". He currently is teaching a number of non-credit classes at the Small Business Development Center in Phoenix, Arizona. He has also participated in numerous radio programs and had a variety of articles published.

He is active in Rotary International, currently President Elect and is on The Board of Directors of the Tempe Rio Salado Club in Arizona.

Martin does presentations and seminars across the country for organizations and associations. The topics he speaks on include; Sales, Customer Service, Marketing and Small Business issues.

▼▼▼▼▼
GUARANTEED RESULTS
▼▼▼▼▼

Order Card For Additional Copies

Yes, I would like _____ additional copies of *Guaranteed Results*. I want them for business associates, employees, friends, relatives, clients, etc.

I have enclosed $13.95 per book plus $3.50 per book shipping and handling.

My total is; Number of books _____ X 13.95
Number of books _____ X 3.50
Total _____

If you would like faster delivery please call or fax your order in. Use your Visa or Mastercard. Include your account number and the expiration date. Please also include your name and phone number in case we have any questions.
Thank you!

▼▼▼▼▼ GUARANTEED RESULTS ▼▼▼▼▼

If You Would Like To Get In Touch With Me!

You can write to me at Robinson & Associates, 12629 North Tatum, Suite 237, Phoenix, AZ 85032. Or you can call me at 1-602-990-1775 or fax me at 1-602-953-3550.

I would very much like to hear from you. If you used one of the tools and it worked, contact me. If you implemented one of the tools and it did not work, contact me. Or maybe you did something different that worked well for you, please tell me about it. As I said in the beginning, this book was written to help you. So thank you for reading *Guaranteed Results* and please tell me what your thoughts are.

You can also contact us to see when we will be doing a program in your area.

Good luck and I hope you generate some great results with the tools that I mentioned.

GUARANTEED RESULTS

Great Books

The E-Myth
by Michael Gerber

Getting Business to Come to You
by Paul and Sarah Edwards

Making It On Your Own
by Paul and Sarah Edwards

Guerrilla Marketing
by Jay Conrad Levinson

Guerrilla Marketing Attach
by Jay Conrad Levinson

The Great Marketing Turn Around
by Stan Rapp & Tom Collins

I-Power
by Martin Edelston

Letters that Sell
by Richard Bayan

Words that Sell
by Richard Bayan

GUARANTEED RESULTS

Puzzle Solution

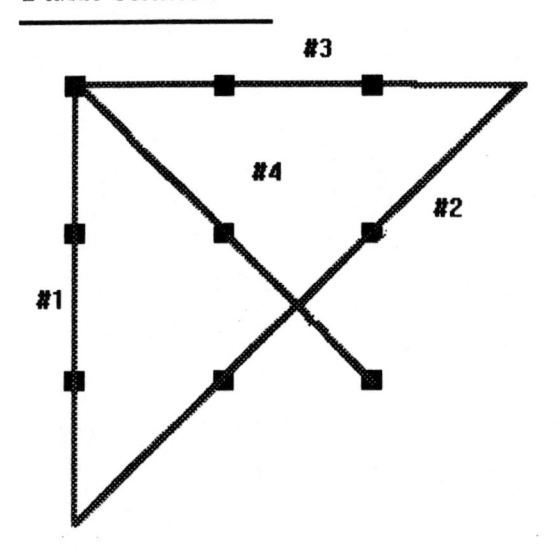

Sometimes you need to think outside the box. You need to expand your thinking and look at all of the possibilities. Too many times we limit ourselves. Open up your mind to all of the possibilities. Marketing can be very frustrating and it can be fun. Keep your mind open to new ideas and give them a try. You may be very pleasantly surprised with how effective it can be.